Together Alone

33 1/3 Global

33 1/3 Global, a series related to but independent from **33 1/3**, takes the format of the original series of short, music-based books and brings the focus to music throughout the world. With initial volumes focusing on Japanese and Brazilian music, the series will also include volumes on the popular music of Australia/Oceania, Europe, Africa, the Middle East, and more.

33 1/3 Japan

Series Editor: Noriko Manabe

Spanning a range of artists and genres – from the 1970s rock of Happy End to techno-pop band Yellow Magic Orchestra, the Shibuya-kei of Cornelius, classic anime series *Cowboy Bebop*, J-Pop/EDM hybrid Perfume, and vocaloid star Hatsune Miku – 33 1/3 Japan is a series devoted to in-depth examination of Japanese popular music of the twentieth and twenty-first centuries.

Published Titles:
Supercell's *Supercell* by Keisuke Yamada
AKB48 by Patrick W. Galbraith and Jason G. Karlin
Yoko Kanno's *Cowboy Bebop Soundtrack* by Rose Bridges
Perfume's *Game* by Patrick St. Michel
Cornelius's *Fantasma* by Martin Roberts
Joe Hisaishi's *My Neighbor Totoro: Soundtrack* by Kunio Hara
Shonen Knife's *Happy Hour* by Brooke McCorkle
Nenes' *Koza Dabasa* by Henry Johnson
Yuming's *The 14th Moon* by Lasse Lehtonen
Toshiko Akiyoshi-Lew Tabackin Big Band's *Kogun* by E. Taylor Atkins
S.O.B.'s *Don't Be Swindle* by Mahon Murphy and Ran Zwigenberg

Forthcoming Titles:
Kohaku Utagassen: The Red and White Song Contest by Shelley Brunt
Yellow Magic Orchestra's *Yellow Magic Orchestra* by Toshiyuki Ohwada

33 1/3 Brazil

Series Editor: Jason Stanyek

Covering the genres of samba, tropicália, rock, hip hop, forró, bossa nova, heavy metal and funk, among others, 33 1/3 Brazil is a series devoted to in-depth examination of the most important Brazilian albums of the twentieth and twenty-first centuries.

Published Titles:
Caetano Veloso's *A Foreign Sound* by Barbara Browning
Tim Maia's *Tim Maia Racional Vols. 1 &2* by Allen Thayer
João Gilberto and Stan Getz's *Getz/Gilberto* by Bryan McCann
Gilberto Gil's *Refazenda* by Marc A. Hertzman
Dona Ivone Lara's *Sorriso Negro* by Mila Burns
Milton Nascimento and Lô Borges's *The Corner Club* by Jonathon Grasse
Racionais MCs' *Sobrevivendo no Inferno* by Derek Pardue
Naná Vasconcelos's *Saudades* by Daniel B. Sharp
Chico Buarque's First *Chico Buarque* by Charles A. Perrone

Forthcoming titles:
Jorge Ben Jor's *África Brasil* by Frederick J. Moehn

33 1/3 Europe

Series Editor: Fabian Holt

Spanning a range of artists and genres, 33 1/3 Europe offers engaging accounts of popular and culturally significant albums of Continental Europe and the North Atlantic from the twentieth and twenty-first centuries.

Published Titles:
Darkthrone's *A Blaze in the Northern Sky* by Ross Hagen
Ivo Papazov's *Balkanology* by Carol Silverman
Heiner Müller and Heiner Goebbels's *Wolokolamsker Chaussee* by Philip V. Bohlman
Modeselektor's *Happy Birthday!* by Sean Nye

Mercyful Fate's *Don't Break the Oath* by Henrik Marstal
Bea Playa's *I'll Be Your Plaything* by Anna Szemere and András Rónai
Various Artists' *DJs do Guetto* by Richard Elliott
Czesław Niemen's *Niemen Enigmatic* by Ewa Mazierska and Mariusz Gradowski
Massada's *Astaganaga* by Lutgard Mutsaers
Los Rodriguez's *Sin Documentos* by Fernán del Val and Héctor Fouce
Édith Piaf's *Récital 1961* by David L. Looseley
Nuovo Canzoniere Italiano's *Bella Ciao* by Jacopo Tomatis
Iannis Xenakis's *Persepolis* by Aram Yardumian
Vopli Vidopliassova's *Tantsi* by Maria Sonevytsky
Amália Rodrigues's *Amália at the Olympia* by Lila Ellen Gray
Ardit Gjebrea's *Projekt Jon* by Nicholas Tochka
Aqua's *Aquarium* by C. C. McKee
J. M. K. E.'s *To the Cold Land* by Brigitta Davidjants
Taco Hemingway's *Jarmark* by Kamila Rymajdo
Einstürzende Neubauten's *Kollaps* by Melle Jan Kromhout and Jan Nieuwenhuis

Forthcoming Titles:
Tripes' *Kefali Gemato Hrisafi* by Dafni Tragaki
Silly's *Februar* by Michael Rauhut
CCCP's *Fedeli Alla Linea's 1964–1985 Affinità-Divergenze Fra Il Compagno Togliatti E Noi Del Conseguimento Della Maggiore Età* by Giacomo Bottà
Sigur Rós' *Ágætis Byrjun* by Tore Størvold

33 1/3 Oceania

Series Editors: Jon Stratton (senior editor) and Jon Dale (specializing in books on albums from Aotearoa/New Zealand)

Spanning a range of artists and genres from Australian Indigenous artists to Maori and Pasifika artists, from Aotearoa/New Zealand noise music to Australian rock, and including music from Papua and other Pacific islands, 33 1/3 Oceania offers exciting accounts of albums that illustrate the wide range of music made in the Oceania region.

Published Titles:
John Farnham's *Whispering Jack* by Graeme Turner
The Church's *Starfish* by Chris Gibson
Regurgitator's *Unit* by Lachlan Goold and Lauren Istvandity
Kylie Minogue's *Kylie* by Adrian Renzo and Liz Giuffre
Alastair Riddell's *Space Waltz* by Ian Chapman
Hunters & Collectors's *Human Frailty* by Jon Stratton
The Front Lawn's *Songs from the Front Lawn* by Matthew Bannister
Bic Runga's *Drive* by Henry Johnson
The Dead C's *Clyma est mort* by Darren Jorgensen
Ed Kuepper's *Honey Steel's Gold* by John Encarnação
Chain's *Toward the Blues* by Peter Beilharz
Hilltop Hoods' *The Calling* by Dianne Rodger
Screamfeeder's *Kitten Licks* by Ben Green and Ian Rogers
The Clean's *Boodle Boodle Boodle* by Geoff Stahl
The Avalanches' *Since I Left You* by Charles Fairchild
John Sangster's *Lord of the Rings, Vols. 1–3* by Bruce Johnson
Soundtrack from *Saturday Night Fever* by Clinton Walker
Eyeliner's *BUY NOW* by Michael Brown
TISM's *Machiavelli and the Four Seasons* by Tyler Jenke

Forthcoming Titles:
The Triffids' *Born Sandy Devotional* by Christina Ballico
5MMM's *Compilation Album of Adelaide Bands 1980* by Collette Snowden
INXS' *Kick* by Lauren Moxey
Sunnyboys' *Sunnyboys* by Stephen Bruel
silverchair's *Frogstomp* by Jay Daniel Thompson
The La De Das' *The Happy Prince* by John Tebbutt
Gary Shearston's *Dingo* by Peter Mills
Kate Ceberano's *Brave* by Panizza Allmark
Robert Forster's *Danger in the Past* by Patrick Chapman
Various Artists' *A Truckload of Sky: The Lost Songs of David McComb* by Glenn D'Cruz
Dinah Lee's *Introducing Dinah Lee* by Kimberly Cannady

The Waifs' *Up All Night* by Rebecca Bennison
The Three Out's *Move* by James Gaunt

33 1/3 South Asia

Series Editor: Natalie Sarrazin

From the films of Bollywood and Lollywood, to home-grown *bhangra* hip-hop, Hindu devotional pop and Sufi rock, Sri Lankan rap, Indo jazz and disco, new-wave electronica and diasporic Asian Underground scene, 33 1/3 South Asia takes readers on a sonically diverse journey through the most significant soundtracks and albums from the twentieth and twenty-first centuries.

Published:
Dil Chahta Hai Soundtrack by Jayson Beaster-Jones
Lata Mangeshkar's *My Favourites, Volume 2* by Anirudha Bhattacharjee and Chandrashekhar Rao
Coke Studio (Season 14) by Rakae Rehman Jamil and Khadija Muzaffar

33 1/3 Africa

Series Editor: Michael Veal

33 1/3 Africa is a series of books on canonical, album-length works of African music including traditional music, experimental music, and, with particular emphasis, popular music. Academic and journalistic writing results in sophisticated, nuanced and accessible narratives on African music.

Published:
Fela Anikulapo-Kuti's *Sorrow Tears and Blood* by Stephanie Shonekan

Forthcoming Titles:
Cesária Évora's *Miss Perfumado* by Jacqueline Georgis
Paul Simon's *Graceland* by Kalvin Schmidt-Rimpler Dinh
Nico, Rochereau, Roger & L'African Fiesta – *Volume 1 (1962–1963)* by Frank Gunderson

Together Alone

Barnaby Smith

Series Editor: Jon Stratton, UniSA Creative, University of South Australia, and Jon Dale, University of Melbourne, Australia

BLOOMSBURY ACADEMIC
NEW YORK • LONDON • OXFORD • NEW DELHI • SYDNEY

BLOOMSBURY ACADEMIC
Bloomsbury Publishing Inc, 1385 Broadway, New York, NY 10018, USA
Bloomsbury Publishing Plc, 50 Bedford Square, London, WC1B 3DP, UK
Bloomsbury Publishing Ireland, 29 Earlsfort Terrace, Dublin 2, D02 AY28, Ireland

BLOOMSBURY, BLOOMSBURY ACADEMIC and the Diana logo
are trademarks of Bloomsbury Publishing Plc

First published in the United States of America 2025
Reprinted in 2025 (twice)

Copyright © Barnaby Smith, 2025

For legal purposes the Acknowledgements on pp.110–111
constitute an extension of this copyright page.

All rights reserved. No part of this publication may be: i) reproduced or
transmitted in any form, electronic or mechanical, including photocopying,
recording or by means of any information storage or retrieval system without
prior permission in writing from the publishers; or ii) used or reproduced in
any way for the training, development or operation of artificial intelligence
(AI) technologies, including generative AI technologies. The rights holders
expressly reserve this publication from the text and data mining exception
as per Article 4(3) of the Digital Single Market Directive (EU) 2019/790.

Bloomsbury Publishing Inc does not have any control over, or responsibility
for, any third-party websites referred to or in this book. All internet addresses
given in this book were correct at the time of going to press. The author and
publisher regret any inconvenience caused if addresses have changed or sites
have ceased to exist, but can accept no responsibility for any such changes.

Whilst every effort has been made to locate copyright holders the publishers
would be grateful to hear from any person(s) not here acknowledged.

Library of Congress Cataloging-in-Publication Data
Names: Smith, Barnaby, author.
Title: Together alone / Barnaby Smith.
Description: New York : Bloomsbury Academic, 2025. |
Series: 33 1/3 Oceania | Includes bibliographical references and index. |
Summary: "Together Alone holds a special place in the hearts of Crowded
House fans and remains one of Neil Finn's boldest musical statements –
and his favourite Crowded House album. Recorded amid the isolated
Karekare wilderness, the album is drenched in mystery and atmosphere,
with songs possessing special qualities that those on other Crowded
House albums – as good as they are – do not. But why exactly are they so
hypnotizing? Featuring first-hand accounts, from Finn and others, the book
also explores the intense circumstances of its recording, its major players, and
other factors including the influence of Maori culture"– Provided by publisher.
Identifiers: LCCN 2024051050 (print) | LCCN 2024051051 (ebook) |
ISBN 9798765105153 (paperback) | ISBN 9798765105160 (hardback) |
ISBN 9798765105177 (epub) | ISBN 9798765105184 (ebook)
Subjects: LCSH: Crowded House (Musical group).
Together alone. | Rock music-Australia-1981-1990-History and criticism. |
Rock music-Australia-1991-2000-History and criticism.
Classification: LCC ML421.C764 S65 2025 (print) |
LCC ML421.C764 (ebook) | DDC 782.42166092/2-dc23/eng/20241105
LC record available at https://lccn.loc.gov/2024051050
LC ebook record available at https://lccn.loc.gov/2024051051

ISBN:	HB:	979-8-7651-0516-0
	PB:	979-8-7651-0515-3
	ePDF:	979-8-7651-0518-4
	eBook:	979-8-7651-0517-7

Series: 33 1/3 Oceania

Typeset by Integra Software Services Pvt. Ltd.
Printed and bound in Great Britain

For product safety related questions contact productsafety@bloomsbury.com.

To find out more about our authors and books, visit www.bloomsbury.com
and sign up for our newsletters.

Contents

Image List x

1 The little phrase: Introduction 1

2 A contrary path: Context and background 13

3 Stay on one string: The (non-Finn) key players 35

4 Ancient streams: At Karekare 51

5 Abstract thought: Song by song 71

6 The alchemy is complete: Aftermath 101

Acknowledgements 110
References 112
Index 120

Image List

3.1 Neil Finn with Youth, Melbourne, 1993. Photo courtesy of Neil Finn private collection 37

4.1 Sea spray moves across the beach at Karekare. Photo: Barnaby Smith 52

4.2 20 Karekare Road as it is today. Photo: Camille Sanson 62

4.3 Mist rolling in just north of Karekare Beach. Photo: Barnaby Smith 70

1 The little phrase: Introduction

The tumble

Karekare is a dangerous place. A misplaced step on a trail, a misjudged tide or a corner taken too fast on a treacherous road can all lead to ruin. One of the many stories from Crowded House's time there recording *Together Alone* involves the English producer Youth almost coming undone in this way. One night, he and the band were walking in darkness along a track with a sheer drop to one side, on the way to the house where they were recording. Lagging behind the rest of the group, Youth, as is his wont, decided to drift from the track into the bush. He promptly lost his footing and fell down the precipice. Luckily, he managed to cling to a branch as he fell, levering himself back to safety. He eventually arrived at the house dishevelled and alarmed, brandishing the stick that saved him. This stick stayed by Youth's side for the rest of the album's recording: a totem and a symbol of the adventure at Karekare.

This incident feels emblematic of the entire project: risky, perilous, a narrow path to tread, a bit of groping around in the dark – but with some kind of enlightenment to be found amid this. Strait is the gate and all that.

The story of *Together Alone*'s creation is by far the most dramatic and fascinating among Crowded House albums. The band faced many challenges in recording it, from an unforgiving physical environment to uncertainty about creative direction and the odd fractious working relationship – all of which made their way into the songs, becoming part of the album's essence.

I have found that listening and responding to *Together Alone* is a little like walking alone on a bush track in the dark, not knowing the safest direction – or even if the safest direction is the best course.

Uncertain form

Describing the experience of being moved by music is perhaps impossible. That momentary physical and emotional frisson is certainly joyous, but this is combined with a stranger, more disorienting feeling that words struggle to capture. It is a strange kind of desire, an unsatisfied need to achieve a certain intangible union with a song or part of a song. It is something I felt most keenly in my teens and early twenties, the time of life when music can be the dominant force in one's being and awareness – the essential substance of identity.

In the difficult task of expressing this unsatisfied urge, I would add that the feeling is a need to 'live' in a song: to inhabit it, to be cocooned within it and in doing so, have it reveal yet more of its secrets and truths. But this is impossible, so it remains a kind of hunger.

This sensation is fleeting. It will not last an entire four-minute song; rather, this moment of transcendence combined with frustration might last only for seconds in response to a particular blend of musical factors. This experience, where time and space seem to evaporate, might be brought on by a melodic sequence, a chord change, or a harmonic or rhythmic element that will come and go in moments. It is all highly subjective, personal and, inevitably, psychological (Stern 2014). It might also be bound up with memory, nostalgia or childhood – one can turn to Marcel Proust's idea of 'involuntary memory' (2006: 308–9) and music's power to trigger such a wistful reaction, with all its exquisite craving.[1]

I'm emphasizing that tingle of unfulfilled desire to be enveloped by, and intimate with, that musical moment.[2] There exists an obscure 1914 poem by the Portuguese writer Fernando Pessoa (1888–1935), titled 'Song', that comes startlingly close to capturing this ethereal and ephemeral sensitivity. Pessoa writes of the 'Remote, uncertain form/ Of what will never be mine', while also describing the titular 'song', with its rare and elusive quality, as 'like someone among trees/Who now shows and now hides' (1982: 30). The poem is a revelation for anyone interested in the emotional effects of music. 'Song' was written forty-four years before Neil Mullane Finn was born in Te Awamutu in 1958, yet the poem aptly describes being transported and overwhelmed by his music.

Across nearly all their studio albums, Crowded House songs offer moments that entrance a listener in this way. It is something British music critic Peter Paphides identified when he wrote the liner notes for the band's 1996 best-of album,

---

[1] Music played a central role in Proust's idea of involuntary memory, as demonstrated by the power of a 'little phrase' in a sonata in *Swann's Way* (Proust [1913] 1970: 159–62). For Proust, music's power lay in its capacity to spontaneously provoke memory, emotion and desire (James 1995) – all Neil Finn staples.

[2] The poet Anne Sexton also sensed this inherent emotional privation in being affected by 'Bachianas Brasileiras No 5 – Aria' by Salli Terri and Laurindo Almeida: 'It makes me cry, like something I've lost. There's something in there that I've lost, that I can't find' (Cody Carvel 2018).

Recurring Dream. 'Crowded House songs possess a defining moment that will stay with you forever,' he writes:

> Sometimes it's hard to put your finger on it, but you certainly know when you've heard it. Remember how those otherworldly first chords to 'Weather With You' chime into view, like a postcard from a distant dream? ... Ah well, you see, that's a Crowded House Moment. As indeed, is the chorus of 'World Where You Live' ... Here's another one. 'Four Seasons In One Day', when those ghostly harmonies converge upon Neil's voice like vultures to a carcass.
>
> (Paphides 1996)

These are all brief sections of songs where Crowded House achieved a sharp and seductive clarity that stands out from, and yet defines, the tracks in question.

However, the songs Paphides cites are, as you would expect given his commentary was for *Recurring Dream*, among the band's most famous and familiar. The points in the songs he mentions are surely memorable to even the casual listener who only hears 'Weather With You' in supermarket aisles (where, in Australia at least, it is likely the song will be on high rotation until the end of time). The Crowded House Moments on *Together Alone* are of a different, more intense kind: cryptic, atmospheric, complex, suggestive, secretive and dark. *Together Alone* is replete with moments that provoke longing for an impossible intimacy.

It is not even the obvious points in these songs: not the choruses, nor any bridge (recurrently the home of some of Finn's most sumptuous passages). The seconds that hypnotize the most are often tucked away in a track's incidental moments. These include the outro for 'Nails in My Feet', where Nick Seymour's single-note, sustained, unresolved bass line lays a platform for Finn's murmured final statement, where it feels like he is talking to himself – about the back door, the stars and so on. Or the unusual coda for 'Catherine Wheels', which departs from the relatively measured first section of this extraordinary track to launch into an unnerving phantasmagoria of surreal imagery, alongside a lightly repetitive acoustic guitar phrase – again powered by a Seymour bass line that pressures the song into untethered, wild territory. The second half of this track is an incantation.

Or the moment in 'In My Command' when a sweeping chord change brings Finn's strident, shouted interlude back to the song's chorus theme (2:17–2:23). Or when he breaks into falsetto towards the end of 'Walking on the Spot'. Or the brief flourish of an unidentified string instrument (possibly synthesized) that fades in to begin the album's closing title track.

Twenty-four hours at 35,000 feet

Together Alone is, thematically, many things. As is typical for Finn, it is an abstract depiction of human relationships in all their fervour and muddiness. It is also, undoubtedly, a 'landscape work'. Therefore, an appreciation of the album is enhanced by an awareness of why Karekare, West Auckland, was selected as the location to create *Together Alone*, and an understanding of this unique place.

Together Alone is Crowded House's fourth studio album of what is now a total of eight. It was their first album to be recorded in Finn's native Aotearoa/New Zealand, and the final studio record they made before his decision to disband the group in 1996. The year or so prior to the commencement of the album's recording, in late 1992, had been exhausting and difficult for the band – even amid critical and commercial success. Their third album, *Woodface*, came out in July 1991 – the LP with all the glossy hits, with their polished and precise pop production, courtesy of long-time collaborator Mitchell Froom: 'Weather With You', 'Fall at Your Feet', 'Four Seasons in One Day', 'It's Only Natural', 'Chocolate Cake'. *Woodface*, regarded by some as the definitive Crowded House album, was an exacting project for the band from start to finish. The process of writing, recording and promoting this record had a substantial bearing on the decision to decamp to rural New Zealand to prepare the next.

The struggles of *Woodface*'s writing and recording are well known among Crowded House fans and need not be dwelled on at length here.[3] The album had inauspicious beginnings when the batch of songs recorded for a follow-up to the excellent but relatively unsuccessful *Temple of Low Men* (1988) was rejected by the band's US label, Capitol, in mid-1990. Sent back to the drawing board, Finn was forced to return to songs written the previous year with his older brother Tim, which were initially intended for a first Finn brothers album. Bringing these songs into the Crowded House fold precipitated Tim joining the group for *Woodface*, a move that, while offering new possibilities for the musical palette, would decisively alter the band's dynamics – particularly on stage. Tim would ultimately (and amicably) leave Crowded House mid-tour in late 1991. While

---

[3] For details of this and a chronicle of Crowded House's first eleven years, see Chris Bourke's *Something So Strong*, still the leading biography of the band.

there was no animosity, this must have led to a degree of disorientation – certainly for Neil.

Along with this were a number of disappointments and missteps in promoting the record. While *Woodface* was successful in the United Kingdom and Europe by any measure, the album did not find particular favour in the United States (where the ubiquitous 'Don't Dream It's Over' had reached number two on the *Billboard* Hot 100 in 1987). Not even 'Weather With You', which reached number seven on the UK singles chart, could penetrate North America. The UK and Europe also took a while to warm up and required a lot of work: the choice of 'Chocolate Cake' as *Woodface*'s first single, a questionable move, got things off on the wrong foot, before the success of 'Weather With You' and an awful lot of touring saw the album peak at number six on the album charts in the UK, where it eventually went double platinum (it also went platinum in Australia).

None of this is very unusual for an ambitious international rock band, but it did take its toll on Finn, Seymour and drummer Paul Hester. The latter in particular, a lover of home comforts, was becoming disillusioned with the treadmill of touring and promotion; a round trip of less than three days from Melbourne to the UK and back, for the band to stagger their way through a dazed performance of 'It's Only Natural' on *Top of the Pops*, was a particularly unpleasant ordeal (Bourke 1997: 239–40).[4]

The two-year journey of *Woodface* altered how Finn saw Crowded House and music-making, resulting in him seeking reconnection with familiar surroundings as well as new artistic

---

[4] During this performance a jetlagged Hester groaned into his mic: 'Twenty-four hours at 35,000 feet!'

impetus. He found both with the making of *Together Alone*, an experience that gave his creative identity a comprehensive overhaul.

The pagan and The Watchman

Finn has acknowledged the sharp contrast between *Together Alone* and its predecessor, *Woodface*. In a 2013 interview to mark the twentieth anniversary of the former's release, he told me:

> [*Together Alone*] is my favourite Crowded House record I think. *Woodface* gets a lot of kudos for being our finest moment, and I'm proud of most of it, but I find it a little overlong and a bit piecemeal. It's a bit of this and a bit of that, whereas *Together Alone* seems like it's got a pretty pervasive atmosphere from beginning to end.
>
> (Interview 2013)

It is worth noting, in the wake of Finn's criticism of *Woodface*'s length, that though it has fewer tracks, *Together Alone*, at 51:32, is actually the longer album.

A confluence of circumstances and intentions makes *Together Alone* what it is: a weighty and impassioned musical statement immersed, as Finn says, in a specific atmosphere. Chief among these is the immediate Karekare landscape that surrounded the large private home the band commandeered for their recording. In the rugged Waitakere Ranges, one is engulfed by rich, dense shades of green; coastal cliffs loom large, bringing a sheerness to the scenery; huge, desolate beaches have the imposing feature of black sand; and craggy rock formations jut out of the water offshore. This setting, along with the variety of meteorological conditions the band encountered during recording, is embedded in each song.

Several other factors were critical in shaping the album's seductive melancholy. One was Crowded House's isolation from not only a music industry that had jaded them in the aftermath of *Woodface*, but also the trappings and comforts of society and culture generally (there was, for example, no television) – even if Auckland CBD was less than an hour's drive away.

Another strong thread on *Together Alone* is the Māori presence and history at Karekare and beyond. This is manifested most prominently on the rousing title track, with its thirty-voice Māori choir, and lyrics based on the Rangi and Papa creation myth that explains the origins of the Māori world. Also important for the album are Māori legends and stories that this location has inspired – such as that of Te Matua (The Watchman), a large rocky headland that sits at the north end of Karekare Beach – and how these correlate with certain lyrical ideas. And it's not just Māori spirituality that contributed. The album's British producer, Martin 'Youth' Glover, was a firm follower of paganism. Crowded House's time at Karekare saw a motley collection of ideas and beliefs converge.

The specific personnel involved were therefore decisive in *Together Alone*'s creation. It was a markedly different team from the one that crafted *Woodface*. Tim Finn had departed. Youth, an eccentric figure known for his background in punk and noise, who to some seemed an odd choice to produce Crowded House, would encourage the band into uncharted musical (and philosophical) territory after three albums with the more conventional Froom. Then there is Mark Hart. The American multi-instrumentalist started working with the band in 1989 and officially joined Crowded House at Karekare.

Hart was critical in defining the textural identity of the record, with his electric guitar, lap steel and keyboards pivotal in the evolution of Crowded House's sound – both for *Together Alone* and beyond.

The final element that makes *Together Alone* so peculiar and original is Finn's altered songwriting compared to previous albums (even if, it should be said, the writing of some songs on *Together Alone* dated back several years). After the sledgehammer sing-alongs of *Woodface*, the songs here offer less predictable structures and fewer anthemic choruses, with Finn approaching composition from an exploratory new angle. Lyrically, *Together Alone* heralded a committed turn towards the complex, the nonlinear, the impressionistic and the fragmented. This darker and weirder sensibility had been adopted a little on *Temple of Low Men*, but now it received free rein. Finn's embrace of abstraction became charged with renewed fervour, combining provocative symbolic imagery with hallucinatory and surreal scenarios suggestive of themes including relationships, alienation, morality and the nature of perception and experience. As stated, this was not unprecedented: from the band's self-titled 1986 debut album onwards, there had been a wilfully ambiguous side to Finn's songs, but on *Together Alone*, his lyrics took on a psychological depth and emotional intensity that expanded Crowded House's literary scope. The circumstances at Karekare were a factor. While most of the album's songs were written in skeletal form prior to arriving at Karekare, Finn and others' imaginations expanded in response to the surroundings, the isolation and the influence of Youth, affecting the course these songs took. The album conjures a sense of place like few others in pop, to the point that in some brief moments one wonders if Karekare itself could be the source of the music. The land is singing, its sonic essence plucked from the ether by Finn and co. and rendered on record. In 'Song', Pessoa writes: 'The groves of pines have, through them / Brushing, shadows and lightest / Breaths of musical rhythms' (1982: 30). It is not inconceivable that Crowded House sensed something similar at Karekare.

This book examines all of this. The album's context and background will be explored, in terms of both the band's circumstances leading up to the making of *Together Alone* and how the record fits into the much wider context of rock and pop history. Finn's approach to *Together Alone* can also be located in the broader sphere of Australasian art, specifically in relation to the decision to record back home in Aotearoa. One chapter will consider Finn's key supporting cast in creating the album (Youth and Hart in particular), while another will attempt to identify the album's qualities and patterns in detail through a song-by-song analysis. A further chapter gives an account of a present-day visit to Karekare. The intention of this trip was to explore and experience the place under the influence of *Together Alone*, noting the effect of the landscape and elements, and 'mapping' Karekare according to the album's lyrics, local influences and the story of its making. In doing so, I came to experiment with the practice of 'psychogeography' – defined, in its simplest terms, as the impact of place on an individual's emotions and behaviour, thereby creating meaning. *Together Alone* is unquestionably an expression of this.

2 A contrary path: Context and background

The wrong side of hip

My CD copy of *Together Alone* is shabby these days. The jewel case is cracked and splintered; the disc itself is worn and scuffed from play. The booklet remains intact, if a little warped and faded. One of the many reasons this copy remains treasured, though, is that Neil Finn signed that booklet when he poked his head out of the stage door of the New Theatre in Oxford, UK, to meet fans after a Crowded House show in June 2010.

I purchased *Together Alone* second-hand around early 1999 from a record fair in the town hall of the same city. I was in my mid-teens and coming late to Crowded House – over two years on from the farewell concert outside Sydney Opera House. Having grown up near Sydney until moving to Britain at age twelve, I had, of course, been aware of the band – largely through the singles from *Woodface* that marked Australian airwaves and charts across 1991–2 – without becoming much of a fan.

There were numerous reasons why I was indifferent to Crowded House until the late 1990s – some to do with personal history, some more to do with culture. The reasons from my end are uninteresting and callow – after parent-instigated obsessions with The Beatles and a few other 1960s acts during childhood, I found myself in a British milieu consumed and blinkered by the dubious merits of so-called Britpop in the mid-1990s. There was little space for Crowded House amid these things.

The wider, more zeitgeist-related reasons I had kept the band at arm's length up to this point reveal one of the more discordant and even unfair chapters in the overall Crowded House story. By the mid-1990s in the UK, when tribalism in music was at a commercially driven frenzied peak, the band had become a byword for middle-of-the-road, inoffensive musical blandness – coffee-table music verging on elevator music. At school, I would sometimes hear insults thrown around: 'I bet you secretly listen to Crowded House' or 'Go home and listen to your Crowded House CDs'. This was perpetuated by the dismissive and occasionally snide attitude towards the band adopted by various quarters of the press.[1] 'We were always on a contrary path from a critical point of view', Finn said in 2013. 'When we started getting good reviews people would always preface it by saying "Well I know I'm not supposed to like Crowded House, but … "' (Interview).

From the vantage point of three decades on, this feels strange, with Finn's kingly status in pop partly achieved because of his more experimental explorations in various musical guises, such as Pajama Club and the Seven Worlds Collide projects. (It was also a view of the band largely confined to the UK, prominent American critic Robert Christgau's infamous antipathy towards Finn notwithstanding.) There are

---

[1] Reviewing Neil Finn's solo album *One Nil* for *NME* in 2001, critic Mark Beaumont described Finn as '[a] man best known for writing beardy REM shite about the weather', concluding with 'red card, you cunt'.

a few explanations for this outmoded view of the band. For one, Crowded House appeared distinctly lacking in image, particularly when compared to the bands that defined the Britpop or grunge movements. This was, it seemed, an all-too 'normal' group of men who were relatable, unthreatening, friendly, goofy. Crowded House seemed an almost family-oriented band whose rock and roll credentials were negligible at a time when the 'edgy' antics of, say, Liam Gallagher made Oasis frequent tabloid fodder.[2] A *New York Times* review of a concert in 1991 stated: 'The group's sweetness and wit are simply too airy for a pop climate absorbed in darkness and aggression' (Holden 1991). A *Melody Maker* review of a London concert in the same year, while positive, noted that the band were 'the wrong side of hip, the wrong side of 30 and come from the wrong side of the world' (1991, cited in Bourke 1997: 201). The fact Princess Diana was reportedly a fan did not help Crowded House's standing in modish circles. (It should not be forgotten that Crowded House did find friends among UK critics in the 1990s, such as Peter Paphides, David Hepworth and Stuart Maconie.[3])

---

[2] This despite the fact the band were prone to loose behaviour: Paul Hester channelled Jim Morrison when, before an encore at a show in Los Angeles in 1991, he marched on stage and proceeded to strip 'bollock naked' as Nick Seymour put it, and simulate self-pleasure (Bourke 1997: 226). There were also multiple cases of fisticuffs between members over the years, including a punch-up between the Finn brothers after a show in Byron Bay.

[3] Indeed *Woodface* received widespread praise upon release. But as the decade wore on, and those more posturing movements (grunge, Britpop) gained stronger traction, the album may have quickly seemed dated.

The music itself also played its part in Crowded House's lack of cool in the 1990s. *Recurring Dream*, the band's mega-selling best-of, was released in 1996. While I owned and appreciated it, this was an album that appeared in the CD collections and car gloveboxes of the middle-aged, middle-class parents of friends, next to white-bread records such as David Gray's *White Ladder* or *The Very Best of Elton John*. The nineteen tracks were undeniably a good snapshot of Finn's gifts, albeit songs with the most commercial bent, but it was a collection engineered for people who saw music as a casual source of entertainment, rather than a passion.

Amid the Britpop landscape and the popular trends of that time in the UK, Crowded House appeared unlikely to inspire fervent devotion – certainly not a band to hang one's identity on, as was the case with acts from Oasis and Blur through to Elastica, Suede and others. If not held in downright disdain by some, they were only in the peripheral awareness of others – and the band even embraced this latter fact with the marketing campaign for *Recurring Dream*. The slogan, 'You know more Crowded House songs than you think you do,' seemed an exercise in damning themselves with faint praise, an admission of their music being catchy but fleeting, pleasant but not layered, decent but not absorbing. This is easily disproven, of course, but it all fed into a climate where my attention was not initially drawn to them.

How does this relate to *Together Alone*, an album that definitively refutes these ideas about Crowded House? The perception of the band as mundane and 'sad' was cemented with *Woodface* – to which *Together Alone* was a reaction. While the singles 'Weather With You', 'Fall at Your Feet', 'Four Seasons in One Day', 'It's Only Natural' and even the maligned

'Chocolate Cake' are all compositional triumphs, these songs are slathered with a production sheen that was firmly aimed at mainstream radio and the charts. Producer Mitchell Froom was undoubtedly perfect for Crowded House on their first two albums, but the songs on *Woodface* hold a polish that, arguably, reduces their vitality. *Woodface* is certainly an album of lyrical acuity and songwriting sophistication, but to listen to it today is to note its staid production – particularly when compared to *Together Alone*.

The previous chapter touched on the practical and promotional difficulties the band endured as they recorded and toured *Woodface*, and how these contributed to Finn's motivation to seek the seclusion of Karekare. But the *Together Alone* project was about more than escaping the music industry: it was the adoption of a new artistic philosophy, as well as a break from certain familiar methods and personnel, in pursuit of a substantially different sound and aesthetic. In retreating to Karekare, and in enlisting Youth, it was as if Finn knew the band had veered a little too close to the grey centre, and that a less conventional approach to many things was required – even if that compromised commercial appeal.[4]

Crowded House's nadir among certain critics and listeners in the 1990s came in the wake of *Woodface* (with a dash of

---

[4] *Woodface* certainly succeeded in bringing Crowded House a broader audience. In the wake of its release, *Vox* declared that the band attracted 'teenyboppers and tactfully-tailored thirty-somethings in equal measure' (Malins 1992, cited in Bourke 1997: 232). A recipe for sales if ever there was one.

'Don't Dream It's Over' maybe). A word often employed in assessments of *Woodface* – from reviews upon release to subsequent retrospective appraisals – is 'charming'. The word implies lightness and surface. *Together Alone* can be regarded as Finn's reaction to things swinging too far towards this dominating pleasantness.

All of this – the falling foul of fashion, the lack of image, the angling for the mainstream with *Woodface* – brings to mind words of the British activist singer-songwriter Leon Rosselson. In a 1982 article, he wrote: 'Rock music is basically conservative … notoriously vulnerable to the whims and fashions of the marketplace.' *Together Alone* was Crowded House's attempt to step outside of this cycle, having been beleaguered by it with *Woodface*, and transcend this conservativeness and brittleness. Rosselson adds that popular music should be 'more deeply rooted in human experience and history than that generated by the rootlessness of urban youth' (cited in Denselow 1989: 210). If nothing else, *Together Alone* is acutely entangled in the chaos and sorrow of human experience (and in its way, history, as later chapters will outline).

Singular vision

Throughout his career, Finn has consistently sought new and innovative ways to stoke the creative fires. At various times, whether in Crowded House or solo, he has made decisions or embarked on projects and collaborations with the aim of stimulating songwriting, attracting the muse and experiencing music in unfamiliar, invigorating settings. This has included embracing unexpected genres and sonic directions, such as the use of loops and samples on the 1998 solo album *Try*

Whistling This or the hybrid of funk, psychedelia and post-punk that was the 2011 self-titled Pajama Club album; left-field collaborations such as that with Wendy Melvoin and Lisa Coleman, once of Prince and the Revolution, on the 2001 solo album *One Nil*; or inclusive and celebratory group projects such as Seven Worlds Collide. Another example might even be partnering with brother Tim in the late 1980s, writing songs in the famous sessions at Murchison Street in Melbourne that would end up on *Woodface*. Joining Fleetwood Mac, too.

These creative manoeuvres have also involved uncompromising and sometimes unpopular decisions on personnel. Finn fired Nick Seymour from Crowded House in 1989 (to be reinstated weeks later) because of perceived 'faltering musical chemistry' (Bourke 1997: 152), while some fans were disappointed when Finn rebooted the band in 2019 without Mark Hart.

All this gives Finn something in common with one of his biggest influences, in terms of both music and philosophy of music, Neil Young, who notoriously would abruptly leave tours, bands and recording projects at crucial times because they were not exciting or inspiring. In a 2014 interview for *The Quietus*, Finn told me, 'The way Neil Young has conducted his career, and his singular vision, I admire probably more than anybody out there.' Finn's creative departures have never seen him behave quite as drastically as Young has, yet both artists are moved by the same curiosity and restlessness that compel them to seek newness and experimentation. Undoubtedly, some of Finn's most significant decisions in pursuit of refreshed inspiration came as Crowded House prepared for their fourth album: the selection of Youth and the resolution to record amid the valleys and cliffs of Karekare.

There is inherent risk in attempting to realize such a 'singular vision' as Finn did with *Together Alone*. The sheer courage it took to record the album this way often feels underplayed in retrospective critiques. Finn could not have known how the isolation would affect the band's chemistry, how they would respond to an extravagant personality such as Youth, and how the technical and practical side of recording would unfold. An Oliver Sacks quote neatly applies to Finn's intent: 'It takes a special energy, over and above one's creative potential, a special audacity or subversiveness, to strike out in a new direction once one is settled. It is a gamble, as all creative projects must be, for the new direction may not turn out to be productive at all' (Sacks 2017: 140).

The decision to record at Karekare, and the place itself, brought a new dimension to Finn's pattern of seeking out stimulation in alternative ways. At several points during Crowded House's initial eleven-year incarnation, Finn became frustrated by the fact that he was the band's sole songwriter and that he alone bore the burden of composing hits and filling out albums (although he certainly found foils in Froom and Tim at various times). This issue contributed to the dismissal of Seymour (Bourke 1997: 153). It also played a part in Finn's decision in 1996 to disband Crowded House (Bourke 1997: 342).

Finn's reaching for different musical experiences, contexts, people and parameters may have been in lieu of a regular songwriting partnership. He sought the friction, feedback, dialogue and exchange of ideas of creative collaboration in these other things. In the absence of a regular, reliable teammate in composing songs, his mind and instincts led him to these experiential ways of giving his creative faculties renewed impetus, providing a certain 'otherness' to balance his own innate sensibilities. Of course, some of these were actual partnerships (let's also not forget his collaboration with The Dixie Chicks on *Time On Earth*'s 'Silent House'), but often they were about-turns stylistically, decisions about musicians and indeed *places*. This is to theorize that Karekare itself – its landscape, seascape and elements – became the creative partner and foil that Finn was seeking, whose absence he had felt so strongly. This is not to personify the terrain in any mystical way, nor suggest that Finn's bond with the landscape was any more meaningful than that held by other figures in *Together Alone*'s recording. Nor is it to imply he was any 'conduit' or 'channel' for nature. But given the dramatic and confronting natural environment, Finn's openness to unfamiliar and alternative stimuli, and the impressions left by the music itself, it is not so far-fetched an idea that Karekare became an authorial voice in its way, and Finn's demanding (and unpredictable) creative partner, on *Together Alone*.

Mantric grooves

Crowded House were by no means pioneers in retreating to a pastoral idyll in pursuit of focus and surroundings conducive to artistry. Over the course of rock history, many dwellings have become integral in the lore of certain albums. Numerous bands are intimately associated with the houses where they gathered to write, rehearse or record, to the point that doing so might be regarded as a rock and roll tradition. Crowded House were adopting a familiar idea and some analogous historical examples are worth considering to place *Together Alone* in a broader context.

A few famous ones immediately come to mind. Led Zeppelin's folk-tinged third album is full of the spirit of Bron-Yr-Aur, the eighteenth-century cottage in Wales where Robert Plant and Jimmy Page decamped to rejuvenate in 1970. There is also The Band's stay at the house named Big Pink, which culminated in the 1968 album *Music from Big Pink*. In an Australasian context, rock band Fraternity's time at Hemming's Farm in the Adelaide Hills is an important part of that group's story, while Kevin Parker recorded Tame Impala's debut 2010 album *Innerspeaker* at Wave House, near Dunsborough, Western Australia.

However, some of the closest spiritual forebears of Crowded House's experiment with *Together Alone* can be found in England in the late 1960s and early 1970s. This time was marked, as Rob Young puts it in *Electric Eden*, by 'an inward exodus, with musicians in pursuit of rural tranquillity' (2010: 45). An example is the influential genre-crossing psychedelic band, Traffic. In 1967, to prepare for their first album *Mr. Fantasy*, the four-piece (which included the great Steve Winwood) descended on rural Berkshire and a dwelling known as 'The Cottage', in the hamlet of Aston Tirrold. Traffic's time here set the tone for the band's entire career, and their single-mindedness in devoting themselves to their craft at The Cottage, despite plenty of psychedelic drugs and tensions between members, demonstrated a focus and work ethic that Finn would likely appreciate. Traffic 'enjoyed total isolation, with not a house, road or pylon in sight' (Young 2010: 285). They also constructed an outdoor concrete stage so they could jam in the sunshine and the twilight. This constant, concentrated and committed playing together was important; as Young puts it, 'The mantric quality of Traffic's grooves – what Winwood called at the time "a constant flow of writing, playing, well, just a flow" – certainly derives its self-perpetuating power from this arrangement' (2010: 286).

'Mantric grooves' and 'flow' are ideas that Youth, who was heavily into concepts like 'energy' and 'vibe', would have prioritized at Karekare. There certainly is a mantric quality to *Together Alone* – 'Kare Kare', 'Fingers of Love', 'Private Universe' and 'Catherine Wheels' being examples – suggesting that Crowded House may have tapped into a similar spirit to that channelled by Traffic at The Cottage. The idea of playing, experimenting, being attentive to surroundings and playing some more, arriving at a certain 'flow', applies to both bands in their respective houses; a certain imprint of texture or arrangement is found across both *Mr. Fantasy* and *Together Alone* (even if Traffic did not record their album in the house).

The wider British folk-rock scene of that period provides further connections, in terms of methods and intentions, with *Together Alone*. Traffic's musical-domestic living arrangement was repeated by Fairport Convention when they gathered at Farley House in Hampshire in 1969.[5] This was another primitive, atmospheric dwelling where nature seemed to encroach and inform the music-making (Young 2010: 258). The band (which featured future Crowded House collaborator Richard Thompson) spent long days here over multiple months writing, arranging and rehearsing material that became *Liege*

---

[5] Fairport Convention's time at Farley House was also a bonding period to process tragedy: Drummer Martin Lamble and Richard Thompson's girlfriend Jeannie Franklyn were both killed when the band's touring van crashed in May 1969.

& *Lief*, another album that drips with the 'mantric grooves' that seem to come from bands' residential experiments.[6]

Another band whose methods suggest a kinship with *Together Alone* is the relatively unheralded Heron. When the folk-oriented four-piece came to record their first album in 1970, they found themselves repelled by the sterility of the standard studio (Young 2010: 288). Instead, they descended on a farmhouse in the Berkshire town of Appleford (very near Aston Tirrold), where they set up to record outdoors in a meadow. The resulting self-titled debut album is steeped in a rural sense of place, thanks to the ambient noises, such as birdsong and wind, picked up by the recordings (Young 2010: 289).

Heron were pioneers in broadening the possibilities of how (and where) popular music might be recorded. A line can be drawn between their innovations and how Crowded House approached *Together Alone* over twenty years later. Indeed, some recording of *Together Alone* took place outside. In an electronic press kit (EPK) created for the album, the band describe setting up outdoors, and Finn and Seymour can be seen in the open air perched on seats with instruments, surrounded by microphones. Youth persuaded Hart to record guitar for 'Pineapple Head' standing in a stone circle on a hill outside the house (Bourke 1997: 252). Much of the album's title track was also recorded outdoors, with some microphones

---

[6] Discussion of albums that are closely associated with a particular dwelling could expand in countless further directions, from Paul McCartney's home recordings for his first two solo albums, through to Justin Vernon's warblings in his Wisconsin cabin for the Bon Iver album, *For Emma, Forever Ago* (2007), via the basement recordings of an outsider musician like Daniel Johnston. Not to mention the ubiquity and sophistication of home recording in the twenty first century.

placed at distant points of the surrounding valley. This was initially to capture the echo of the log drums, but also caught, Paul Hester said, 'all the birds and bugs and insects ... buzzing in time with the rhythm of the drums' (Green 2016a). This very much corresponds with Heron's *modus operandi*. The same spirit of simplicity or even innocence may have been in play when the band recorded takes of 'In My Command' in the nude (Bourke 1997: 251).

Sense of occasion

These bands were looking for some kind of retreat or distance – whether from a physical environment such as a city, or certain responsibilities, distractions or temptations. However, none of these experiments in 'destination inspiration' occurred in a place that was especially remote. Civilization was just down the road in each case: Bron-Yr-Aur is close to Aberystwyth; both Traffic's Aston Tirrold and Heron's Appleford are near the cities of Oxford and Reading; Tame Impala's Wave House is a short drive from the holiday town of Dunsborough. At Nigel and Jody Horrocks's house at Karekare, Crowded House were less than an hour's drive from Auckland CBD – the band relied on the West Auckland suburb of Henderson for supplies and would sometimes take time out from recording to visit the city. They were not seeking the back of beyond.

The isolation of Karekare should therefore not be overstated – even if Crowded House's isolation was of a somewhat different kind from the other examples given, simply because it was in New Zealand, so far removed from the Northern Hemisphere's traditional music industry centres. None of the aforementioned bands were necessarily trying to escape from society, culture or people generally, and this was not really the case for Crowded House.

The question of remoteness relates more to intention than actual distance from towns and cities and the wider world. Even Henry David Thoreau, when at Walden Pond between 1845 and 1847, was within walking distance of the town of Concord and relatively close to Boston – his experiment in 'wilderness' was defined by intention rather than specific location. For Crowded House, and most of these bands, the intention can be summarized as a focused, concentrated and collaborative creative effort in a countryside locale where the natural world is an immediate inspiration (as well as a practical reality to be managed).

While this was the overriding motivation for Finn, there were other factors in play too that went beyond just the musical mission. He was also hoping to provide a landmark, formative moment in the band members' lives, one that would grant new knowledge and indelible memories. Finn said:

> We wanted to create a unique experience for ourselves and for these two wastrels from Brixton [Youth and engineer Greg Hunter], something that we would remember for the rest of our lives, we'd tell our children about, something that no one else had ever had … It wasn't the idea of getting really relaxed and beachy, it was the idea of getting caught up in the elements.
>
> (Green 2016a)

He was aiming for a 'sense of occasion' for all involved (Interview 2013). Hester observed: 'The actual recording or making the music was a little bit of an interlude… sometimes', and Finn said the period transcended being 'just a job at work to make an album, it [was] more of an all-round sensory experience. It'll be more special for us than whatever ends up happening to the record, this time is etched into our souls' (Green 2016a).

There is more to it still, beyond the 'sense of occasion' and the bid to escape distractions. Finn's ideas about making this a project based around responding to the landscape also define the Karekare period as Crowded House's own experiment in a kind of rural psychogeography. This is, essentially, where the individual 'reads' their surroundings to form identity, community, spirituality or, in this case, art (which revisits the idea of Karekare as Finn's creative foil). Guy Debord, the French situationist philosopher who conceived the concept, defined psychogeography as 'the specific effects of the geographical environment, consciously organized or not, on the emotions and behavior of individuals' (Debord 1955).[7] These words are highly germane to Crowded House's time at Karekare. Indeed, popular music scholar Tony Mitchell writes that the song 'Kare Kare' 'celebrates a psychogeographic attachment to the eponymous beach on the west coast of Auckland' (2009: 148). Chapter 4 will recount a psychogeography-directed visit to Karekare, and consider how *Together Alone* might inform that experience.

Migratory birds

The decision to record at Karekare was also an effort to recalibrate the band after the draining period of promoting *Woodface* – Hester's commitment, in particular, was wavering

---

[7] Debord was applying psychogeography to an urban environment, specifically Paris, but scholarship has emerged since that considers the concept in relation to a rural environment too (Overall 2016).

following heavy touring. Another significant factor was Finn's desire to reconnect with New Zealand.

By 1992, Finn had not lived in the country for roughly a decade, with Crowded House being predominantly based in Melbourne when not touring elsewhere or recording in Los Angeles. But in April of that year, the band toured New Zealand and Finn noticed a buzz in the air as the nation emerged from a recession that had peaked the previous year (Bourke 1997: 246). He had also never recorded in New Zealand before. He told the BBC at the time, 'I just looked longingly at the country and thought, damn it – this is a really inspiring place, why don't we record here?' (Bourke 1997: 246).

And in 2013:

> We had been back in New Zealand on tour and been driven around the country, and it was beautiful weather, and I fell in love with the place again and got fresh enthusiasm for the land and the light. We'd been coming and going that whole time living in Melbourne. I can't remember the single moment it dawned on me to make a record there, but we had that notion and I went looking for a place.
>
> (Interview)

It is not clear exactly how much of a say the rest of the band had in the decision – though, given Hester's predilection for domestic comforts and Seymour's love of city life, there may have been a raised eyebrow or two on their part.

Finn's urge to return to Aotearoa for creative reasons might be placed in a tradition of Australasian artists acting on a similar pull. It begins with a phenomenon that almost goes without saying: over the last century and more, writers, artists and musicians in Australia and New Zealand have consistently felt the need to leave their homeland to both develop their practice and access opportunities (though this cultural brain drain is less pronounced today). Crowded House's mission has always been inherently global, given the demands on a major-label rock band, not to mention the international make-up of the group. Finn certainly qualifies as part of this diaspora: an artist from Down Under apparently outgrowing their own backyard and needing to expand their creative capacities by relocating to overseas.

History is littered with artists from Australia or New Zealand who left for Europe or the United States and never returned to live. However, a childhood in Australia or New Zealand, particularly a rural or semi-rural one, is something that can stay with you in a latent but ingrained way after you leave, ultimately creating a dreamy, romantic and seductive remembered world in one's imagination (as I can attest). Certain expat Australasian artists with a particularly broad-minded vision, a poetic sensibility perhaps informed by childhood and memory in this way, did return (and Finn counts among these).

Take, for example, the novelist Patrick White (1912–90), who initially left Australia for school in England and then spent fourteen years away during early adulthood, mostly in the United Kingdom but also in the United States, Greece and Egypt. By the end of this period away from Australia, a passion for his homeland's landscape had been rekindled (partly due to time spent in Greece, which reminded him of Australia [Marr 1991: 238]). He returned to Sydney in 1947 and, while holding reservations about Australian society, regarded his perceptions of Australian conditions and Australian life as integral to his literary imagination. Several visual artists have trodden a similar geo-cultural path: in particular, Fred Williams (1927–82) and Arthur Boyd (1920–99), both of whom returned to Australia after long stints in London with a rejuvenated appreciation and excitement at the artistic possibilities of the country's environment.

A further example is Aotearoa author Janet Frame (1924–2004), whose semi-autobiographical, posthumously published novel *Towards Another Summer* is a meditation on longing for the New Zealand landscape of childhood and memory. It is the story of a London-based New Zealand writer who describes herself as a 'migratory bird' (Frame [2007] 2009: 7) as she considers her divided sense of belonging. The novel sees Frame evaluating her identity as it relates to the concepts of home and exile. Her missing the 'snowgrass and snowberries and tussock … of the Southern Alps' (Moorhouse 2008), along with grief over the death of her father, precipitated her return to New Zealand in 1963 after seven years in the UK. She described New Zealand as 'the country where one first saw daylight and the sun and the dark' (Frame 1985: 151).[8]

Finn's reasons for returning to New Zealand to record mark him as distinct from all these examples in some way. Of course, Finn has lived in an age when the tyranny of distance is less stark due to advances in both inter-hemispheric travel and communication technology. His return, initially for an extended visit, was not quite the same life-changing decision it would have been for White, Frame and co. However, there is likely a specific emotional charge, driven by a psycho-poetic bond with his homeland, that unites Finn with such figures. His reconnection with New Zealand is in the spirit

---

[8] A further possible link between Finn and Frame comes with the fact a single released by the reformed Crowded House in 2021 was called 'To the Island' – echoing the title of Frame's 1982 work, *To the Is-land*.

of these artists and writers – he was triggered by memory, personal history and maybe a mild homesickness to explore its inspirational possibilities. Shortly after the recording of *Together Alone* was wrapped, Finn bought property in Auckland and based himself there with his family (Bourke 1997: 281).

It is sometimes said that you achieve a clearer view of your home country while away from it, and this is arguably especially true when that home country is New Zealand or Australia, due to the distances often involved (and perhaps the historical colonial identity). Finn's extended time spent traversing the globe allowed New Zealand to dance seductively in the corners of his imagination, giving him a perspective that recognized the landscape's immense potential for feeding his particular mode of melodic and lyrical expression. To paraphrase Frame, he sensed the magnetism of the first place he saw the daylight, the sun and the dark.

The grey bunker

Given the preparation and logistics involved in organizing to record at Karekare, it all came together remarkably quickly. Having decided in mid-1992 to record in New Zealand, Finn soon honed the plan by rejecting the idea of a conventional, established studio and resolved to rent a house and install one. The month-long search for a property became a minor adventure that took Finn to various parts of the North Island (Bourke 1997: 246) – an endeavour that, one would imagine, consolidated his re-energized passion for New Zealand.

'In the course of looking for a place, I looked on Great Barrier Island, all around Piha, Karekare, quite a lot of places,' said Finn in 2013. It so happened that English singer, instrumentalist and composer Jaz Coleman, once a bandmate of Youth's in Killing Joke, was at the time living on Great Barrier Island, 100 kilometres to the northeast of Auckland. Finn visited Coleman who showed him a 'little shack' that had no power (Interview 2013). Deeming this option a little too rustic, Finn turned his attention to the West Auckland coastline. Among the properties inspected in this region was 20 Karekare Road, then owned by music producer Nigel Horrocks and his wife Jody Horrocks. The house was 'a stark concrete structure, nestled in the side of a hill like a gun-metal grey bunker' (Bourke 1997: 247). Indeed, photographs and footage from the time do show a building reminiscent of the batteries, blockhouses and pillboxes that defended coastlines during the Second World War. Features included floor-to-ceiling windows in a large living room that opened to the valley that, to use architectural shorthand, 'brought the outdoors in', and a bush track that led to Karekare Beach.

The property has an illustrious history. Horrocks bought the land in 1983 from none other than Sir Edmund Hillary (Hepburn 2011), who co-owned, with fellow mountaineer Mike Gill, a significant amount of land around Karekare in the 1970s (*Stuff* 2009). Horrocks built the house in 1986, adhering to 'traditional methods' (Wynn 2011); it was designed by renowned New Zealand architect Andrew Patterson (then a student) and included a sheltered amphitheatre in the backyard, one of several nods to classical Greek design (Hepburn 2011).

Both before and after Crowded House's time at the house (which is now known as Ahu Ahu House and is a holiday rental), Horrocks embraced its use in various show business projects. In the autumn of 1992, the film *The Piano*, directed by Wellington-born Jane Campion, was shot around Piha and Karekare. Actor Harvey Keitel stayed at Horrocks's house during filming (Bourke

1997: 247). Radiohead also visited in the late 1990s and even considered recording their follow-up to *OK Computer* at the house (*NME* 1997). In the 1990s and 2000s, Horrocks pursued the idea of his house as a recording destination and reportedly also welcomed Pearl Jam and Portishead, among others, to Karekare (*Pro Audio Asia* 2009).

For Crowded House's recording, a temporary movable wall was erected in the living area to separate the main recording space from the control room, while various rooms and domestic spaces were converted into booths and editing suites. Recording equipment from Auckland's Revolver studio was painstakingly transported up a rugged approach and driveway. A baby grand piano had to be installed. A mixing desk's passage up the driveway was perilous. Other gear was craned in, while Horrocks and the band collaborated on installing a bridge, and even a road was laid (Bourke 1997: 248).

Initially, the accommodation arrangements had the four-piece band ensconced together at another house a short walk away (Bourke 1997: 248). However, as Hester put it, 'We all moved out from the one house, slowly everyone went, "Oh, I've gotta get my own place"' (Green 2016a). Band members scattered to their own rented digs.

The recording of *Together Alone* at Karekare took place across the final couple of months of 1992 and into January 1993. It was the warm summer months with their long days and intensity of light, which, along with the landscape, the colourful mix of people, the weather, the isolation and the house, ensured, as Finn said, 'a great sense of atmosphere on the record that probably wouldn't have come about any other way' (Interview 2013).

3 Stay on one string: The (non-Finn) key players

The question of what constituent parts make up Crowded House's overall identity is not as straightforward as it might seem. Of course, the band's musical substance, in all aspects, is dominated by Neil Finn. His initial vision birthed the band, and his melodic and harmonic temperament and lyrical landscape have captivated listeners worldwide. That said, Crowded House have always been, and remain, more than simply a vehicle for Finn's songs – and it is worth considering the other figures who have informed the group's collective personality and spirit.

Nick Seymour and Paul Hester's presence and prowess as studio musicians, and their capacity to put their own stamp on songs, grew as the band evolved during its initial eleven-year incarnation – to the point that *Together Alone* is their apogee as players. The album saw them taking risks, exploring their range and becoming more interactive, improvisatory performers. Of course, Hester had also contributed as a songwriter prior to *Together Alone* – 'Italian Plastic' on *Woodface* being one example, 'My Telly's Gone Bung', recorded in 1989 but not released until 1999's *Afterglow* compilation, another. Seymour, meanwhile, had provided some prominent bass parts on several major songs, in particular 'Don't Dream It's Over', 'Hole in the River' and 'Whispers and Moans'. But on *Together Alone* their musical traits are more singularly discernible, both within individual songs and across the whole record (and there were certain reasons – and people – behind this, which this chapter will address).

On stage, a different dynamic was in play. In the 1980s and 1990s, Seymour and Hester were major contributors to the band's flamboyance and charm as a live act. The banter between the three members, and with the audience, became one of the most adored characteristics of Crowded House, with Hester's occasionally extreme on-stage behaviour becoming the stuff of legend. From the earliest days, the drummer was especially loved by fans, thanks in part to these antics.

Other figures who have made distinguished contributions to the Crowded House endeavour prior to *Together Alone* included Mitchell Froom, keyboardist Eddie Rayner, Tim Finn and recording engineer Tchad Blake. The band has always been a cast of talents and personalities lending support and colour to Finn's songs, whether that be a tasteful organ solo in the studio (Froom) or feigning masturbation while naked on stage (Hester). It is therefore important to acknowledge two contrasting individuals who made a transformative impact during the making of *Together Alone*, and who altered Crowded House's DNA: Youth and Mark Hart.

A photo of Finn and Youth was taken in Melbourne in 1993 (Figure 3.1). Finn is holding a mug of something and looks into the camera with a neutral, slightly nonplussed expression. He is wearing a dark grey shirt. Youth, on the other hand, is wincing a little as he assumes a more theatrical demeanour. His fingers clutch what appears to be a fairly large lit joint, while his other hand is raised in a gesture that is part wave, part 'no photos'. He is wearing a floral shirt, a beaded necklace and sports flowing long hair.

Figure 3.1 *Neil Finn with Youth, Melbourne, 1993. Photo courtesy of Neil Finn private collection.*

This image neatly encapsulates the differences between the two most influential people in the *Together Alone* project: the focused, structured pragmatist and the mercurial, cryptic and spontaneous maverick with a penchant for mysticism. The two months of recording at Karekare involved a disparate concoction of styles and values. Despite some difficult moments as conflicting personalities collided (that went beyond just Finn and Youth), 'somehow it worked' (Finn, in Bourke 1997: 256).

Youth is a compelling character in the Crowded House story (the line 'Produced by Youth' in the credits was a mysterious detail when I first encountered *Together Alone*). His emergence came as a result of the band's growing desire for different methods, philosophies and intensity in the studio. Mention his name to the average informed music fan today, especially in the UK, and he is known as the bass player from Killing Joke, a collaborator with Paul McCartney in the experimental project The Fireman, and an esteemed producer with a vast and eclectic list of credits – probably in that order.

Born in 1960,[1] by the time he was enlisted to produce *Together Alone* in 1992, Youth had enjoyed a whirlwind career. He joined his first band in 1977, before the formation of Killing Joke in 1979. The band's urgent, experimental and visionary fusion of punk, funk and dub/reggae quickly made them a favourite of authoritative tastemaker, the BBC radio DJ John Peel, bestowing on them lasting credibility. Youth left Killing Joke in 1982, having made three muscular and ambitious albums (he has reunited with the band multiple times since). The self-titled first of these is regarded as a pivotal moment in early post-punk. After Killing Joke, Youth's work expanded in many directions. His early production credits included goth-rock band Alien Sex Fiend and synth-pop pioneers Erasure, while in 1986 he released an album with a new band, Brilliant, which featured Jimmy Cauty, who would go on to co-found The KLF and The Orb. Youth's appeal to Crowded House in 1992 was primarily due to his reputation as a producer of dance and techno music (Bourke 1997: 244), although in the late 1980s and early 1990s he also took on some major album production projects in the pop realm, such as Bananarama's *Pop Life* and Yazz's *Wanted*.

If all this does not sound particularly Crowded House-y ('nothing Youth had done in music suggested it was a good idea,' wrote Bourke [1997: 245]), that is precisely why Finn was drawn to this colourful figure over options such as Gil Norton, Steve Lillywhite and John Leckie. 'He wasn't like any of

---

[1] Youth was born Martin Glover. The nickname was the result of his devotion to the Jamaican deejay, Big Youth.

the other producers we met at the time,' said Finn. 'He spoke about music in a refreshing way, and he had his foot in a few different camps. Killing Joke were enormously heavy, not that we were particularly big fans, [but we also] liked the fact he had a very keen pop sensibility' (Interview 2013). Finn has also described Youth as a 'wildcard', a 'leftfield choice' and a 'more adventurous decision ... than the more predictable Steve Lillywhite' (Neilfinn.com 2016).

Or the more predictable Mitchell Froom:

> [Youth] wasn't like Mitchell Froom, who was very studious and a wonderful producer in that sense. He was very detailed and worked the songs out to get them tight as; if you've got a problem, [he'll] come in with a solution the next day. Youth was much more abstract in his terminology, but we thought it was a good time to have somebody like that, as we were determined to make an album that was looser and more sprawling and a bit more psychedelic than the last thing we'd done, and he seemed like an apt choice.
>
> (Interview 2013)

This is not to suggest necessarily that Froom was incapable of innovation and spontaneity. Not engaging the American for *Together Alone* was more about breaking with familiarity than breaking with Froom.

For Youth's part, it is hard to gauge exactly how much knowledge he had of Crowded House prior to their approach. He would probably have known *Woodface*, or at least its hit singles, and maybe 'Don't Dream It's Over' from its success in the United States. Following the completion of *Together Alone* and observing that Youth ultimately did not take the 'psychedelic' aesthetic far enough, Finn said, 'I don't think he really wanted to be known as the guy who screwed up

Crowded House' (Bourke 1997: 256), which suggests Youth was aware – or became aware – of audience perceptions and expectations of the band.

The first meeting between Youth and Crowded House is a well-known anecdote and involved Finn, Seymour and Hester visiting the producer at his home in Brixton, South London. Finn's impression of Youth on that occasion was as 'an alternative lifestyler, an escapee from Glastonbury, but within that there was keen intelligence' (Interview 2013). Two things in particular impressed: Youth's ability to roll a resplendent joint and his record collection, a perusal of which led to discussion of potential directions for the new album – David Bowie and the Velvet Underground being particular reference points. Youth's musical sensibility was defined by eclecticism, enthusiasm and deep knowledge. His innate understanding of – and love for – pop idioms was matched by a devotion to historical obscurities and contemporary underground trends.

This should dispel any idea that Youth was ill-equipped to work with Crowded House, or that he had no predilection or expertise regarding the singer-songwriter, or melody and balladry. Let's not forget the McCartney association when considering this question (the first album by The Fireman was created a matter of weeks before Youth left for New Zealand) and note that while at Karekare, Youth had Cat Stevens's *Tea for the Tillerman* on heavy rotation (Bourke 1997: 249). He had also produced the 1992 album *Seven* by James, a band broadly speaking occupying the same melodic rock-pop terrain as Crowded House in the early 1990s. He even co-wrote and produced the ubiquitously popular, rather twee song 'Sunshine on a Rainy Day', made famous by Zoë. With these details in mind, the choice of Youth does not seem such a wild and risky one after all.

In a 2009 interview, Youth gave his thoughts on why he was selected as producer. Expressing some surprise at his appointment ('It was an amazing break they chose me. I think they were looking for a challenge'), he acknowledged that it was his vast record collection that ultimately won the band over: 'I can totally understand that – how that can make it all make sense and it have absolutely nothing to do with whether I can knob-twiddle or whatever' (Doyle). Sensibility, chemistry and unpredictability were what Crowded House saw in Youth. The band were also attracted to him because of his wilful obliviousness to musical boundaries, which he duly demonstrated at Karekare.

There was another side of him that made an impact. Youth described enduring an LSD-induced existential crisis in his early twenties in the early 1980s: an 'epiphany or illumination … that was very acid-drenched'. Youth endured 'a breakdown, having my ego shredded' (Garland 2016), precipitating a spiritual journey that led him to a version of paganism, and he became a druid. So Youth arrived at Karekare equipped with a collection of crystals, burying them around the place and using them in various group situations.[2] He also held court about spiritual matters over meals, which grew a little tedious for some band members (Bourke 1997: 255); encouraged everyone to go barefoot; and in general allowed his esoteric leanings full expression. Finn recalls him walking around the property with his precious, life-saving stick shouting 'Pagan! Pagan!' when recording sessions were gaining momentum.

---

[2] Crystals are employed in several ways in paganism and druidry, from ritual use in practices such as divination (known as 'crystallomancy') to their use in healing and more. Burying them in the earth is said to 'charge' them.

> It was his form of encouragement. He was into crystals and all the hallmarks of the pagan thing. I was pretty cynical and sceptical about all that stuff; it wasn't a spiritual journey for me at all. I found it amusing, to be honest. I'm not putting shit on it for what might be a very keenly held belief, but I didn't relate to it, although I kind of enjoyed it because it added a certain theatre to things. He was all about ley lines, and he buried crystals down by the waterfall, and then forgot where they were and couldn't find them because he was so stoned. He was conscious of all the energy of the landscape – I took it as an affirmation of what we were doing, but I wasn't particularly buying into it.
>
> (Interview 2013)

Youth was an extravagant, abstruse personality. Finn and Hester have given amusing impressions of him over the years, mimicking his characteristic South London brogue. Based on these, Youth seems like a version of Danny from the cult film *Withnail & I* – the drug-engorged waster who believes head hair is an aerial that picks up cosmic signals.

Youth's paganistic and pantheistic sensibilities did not really make their way onto *Together Alone* in any discernible way – maybe because he ran into Finn's scepticism, or maybe because Youth only intended a focus on spirituality to be part of the experience at Karekare, rather than the music itself. So how exactly should Youth's undoubtedly large contribution to *Together Alone* be defined? It is difficult to be specific about the nature of his approach, because so much about his approach was not specific. It becomes harder still to pinpoint when you consider his insistence that when producing he consciously attempts to have minimal influence on an album's abiding feel. In 2023, he said, 'I try to be as invisible as I can ... One of the reasons I've had a lot of longevity as a producer is that I've never really had a "Youth" sound. I try and find the sound that's right for the artist' (*Made By Music*).

Granted, this is likely true of many producers to varying extents – including someone like Froom – but Youth's approach at Karekare was almost radically hands-off, at least in terms of the musical, technical, or structural aspects of songs or arrangements. For *Together Alone*, Youth prioritized ambience and atmosphere – and given these are things for which the album is celebrated, his contribution is to be admired, even if Finn has described his methods as 'sometimes a little vague' (Interview 2013), and there were some antagonistic moments between band and producer during recording. Hart said: 'As far as being a competent nuts-and-bolts producer, he was up in the stars somewhere. And that appealed ... in many ways, because Mitchell is very much a tight-fisted, cracking-the-whip kind of guy. With Youth, it's like "making a record should be like ... making a journey"' (Bourke 1997: 245).

To ensure that the period at Karekare was indeed a 'journey', Youth arrived with a head full of ideas. He regarded himself as a facilitator for bonding and team-building, a 'coach' for group dynamics, almost a guide for personal and relationship development – albeit with a firmly psychedelic bent. He introduced, in his words, 'some fairly radical ideas of how to approach creativity in different ways, using different headsets and psychologies to bond the group' (Doyle 2009). The idea was to '[set up] atmospheres in which the band could capture certain feels' (Bourke 1997: 250). To achieve this, Youth led the band into novel and experimental territory, including the

Heron-like outdoor recording, singing while clutching crystals, and indeed 'nude night'.[3]

Another appealing feature of Youth's production style was that he had little time for virtuosity or noodling – a focus on simplicity was one of his key contributions. This can be heard in several of the album's most expressive passages; whenever there is an instance of a particular note, refrain or idea repeating or sustaining itself in an ear-catching way as the architecture of a song transforms around it, that is probably Youth's influence. The held, repeated B♭ played by Seymour on bass that heralds the outro to 'Nails in My Feet' is one example (2:54–3:04); the ringing lead electric guitar towards the end of 'Locked Out' is another (2:36–2:50: a 'one-note guitar solo', to invoke Neil Young); as is Hester's fantastically hypnotic drumming as 'Kare Kare' reaches its climax (2:40–3:23). 'He'd just encourage us to keep playing,' said Finn, 'and then encourage Nick to stay on one string rather than playing this frilly stuff everywhere – "Stay on one string, man!" – and listen out for good jammy moments and encourage us to be as loose as we could' (Interview 2013).

The art of jamming is one area where Youth and Crowded House enjoyed a particularly good fit. In Youth, they encountered a producer who was not only encouraging of jamming, but likely saw it as another way to foster group bonds. These sessions would sprawl, stop and start, sometimes without much focus, often very late at night, as Youth spurred them on to find inspiration in improvisation. And they did: 'Kare

---

[3] There are conflicting accounts of the details regarding the band's dalliance with naturism. Bourke states that going nude was Hester's suggestion, and that the song in question was 'In My Command'. Youth has implied it was his idea, and that the song was 'Locked Out' (Doyle 2009).

Kare', credited to the whole band, grew out of a jam, as did the wonderful coda for 'Catherine Wheels'. Eighteen months of touring *Woodface* had developed Crowded House into a formidable jam band when performing live. The expectation was that Youth would take it further and allow this side of the group to be expressed in the studio. '*Together Alone* represented probably the only point where we jammed on record,' said Finn (Interview 2013).

Another of Youth's key impacts on the album was his encouragement of band members to have increased agency and control over their own contributions; the 'nuts and bolts' that he abstained from became the domain of Crowded House's individuals. 'We were all actually playing the parts we thought of, instead of having parts imposed upon us,' said Seymour (Bourke 1997: 250). When it came to the famous day recording the album's title track with the Te Waka Huia Cultural Group Choir, Cook Islands log drummers and brass band – a major musical and logistical undertaking – Youth largely left Crowded House to their own devices in coordinating musicians, composing parts and conducting. Clearly, he believed that insisting the band take creative leadership on this central song was crucial in ensuring its vision was realized.

Youth also had the effect of coaxing out certain untapped qualities of musicianship in the band. Hester, in particular, responded to the producer's experience and preferences brought from dance music (Youth is known as a pioneer of genres such as psytrance). 'We quite liked the idea of being deconstructed by someone from club culture,' said Finn, while Seymour emphasized Youth's proclivity for 'live mixing from DJ or house culture' during recording. '[T]hat really assisted Paul,' Seymour added, 'I really feel that even though Paul struggled with Youth on occasion, he saw that side of seeing drums texturally' (Neilfinn.com 2016).

Hester's drumming and percussion on *Together Alone* take a noticeable cue from psychedelic rock, and even drone or acid house. The aforementioned passage in 'Kare Kare' is an example of this 'textural' approach. His work on 'Private Universe' in partnership with the log drummers also demonstrates this new propensity towards hypnotic, mantric percussion – and this is in part thanks to Youth's influence. Seymour, too, has described a kind of epiphany during the recording of *Together Alone*, saying, 'I really believe I found something, realizing that my instrument was bass; I went to the next level on that record, I think, as a bass player' (Neilfinn.com 2016).

Then there is Hart. Youth 'brought the normally reticent Hart out of himself' (Bourke 1997: 255), leading to the improbable performance by this demure Midwesterner of a 'rap' that begins and ends the Hester song 'Skin Feeling'. It is hard to picture Hart spouting those spontaneous lines about rolling in the sand, flying like an eagle and swimming in the ocean like a fish.

Hart first played with Crowded House when the three-piece were touring *Temple of Low Men* in the United States across 1988–9, filling in on keyboard. Up to that point, his most notable credit had been as a member of Supertramp, although more interesting were the band Combonation, for whom Hart played guitar and keys; the five-piece had a touch of late-period Split Enz to their agile new-wave pop, though they didn't last beyond one album.

Hart was immediately a good fit with Crowded House. A studious and placid presence, his phlegmatic nature ensured he did not disrupt the established on-stage chemistry between Finn, Seymour and Hester. He was initially asked to join the band officially in 1989, only for the idea to be nixed by Froom, but was recalled for the *Woodface* tour in 1991 because the band were not clicking with Tim Finn on keyboards (who left the band soon after). As the Karekare sessions commenced, he was still not formally part of Crowded House – Finn invited him to become the fourth member in early December 1992, and over the following two months and beyond Hart made instrumental contributions that came to define *Together Alone*.

'It's hard to be specific because he was bedded into the band at that point,' said Finn when asked about Hart's work on the album, 'but it gave a broader palette when we were imagining things. Mark's a good presence – steady, positive, quite funny in an underplayed way' (Interview 2013). It may have been difficult for Finn to identify the specifics of Hart's input, but for listeners it is more obvious. His electric guitar on 'Fingers of Love' gives the song an immense scale, cathedral-like in scope; his solo (2.16–2.33) adheres to Youth's belief in simplicity and 'keeping to one string', whilst also being probably the most elaborate and florid instrumental passage on the album. Hart's twelve-string has a more decorative and accented presence on 'Distant Sun', while 'Nails in My Feet' is another display of his soloing dexterity, a more understated performance (1.22–1.44) that is beautifully paced and defined by its striking pauses.

Hart's presence as a second guitarist also allowed Finn less responsibility and more freedom with his own playing. 'With both of us playing guitar on all of the tracks, it was really good for me, because I'm used to having to hold the chords down and sing at the same time – the sound was just fuller immediately,' Finn said (Green 2016a). This 'fuller' sound is evident throughout the album, but the two guitarists in complementary tandem are most conspicuous on the louder, more frenetic tracks: 'Locked Out', with its two layers of electric guitar, stands out, as do 'In My Command' and 'Black and White Boy'.

One point Finn *has* made about Hart is that he 'really learned how to play lap steel guitar on [*Together Alone*] and that became a signature sound for us, and for him' (Neilfinn.com 2016). The crowning demonstration of Hart's lap steel work is 'Private Universe', though the instrument is also responsible for the ghostly chimes at the beginning of the opening track 'Kare Kare', which beautifully establish the album's tone. His sensitive mandolin on 'Pineapple Head' is also worth appreciating, as are his compositional contributions: Hart played a minor role in the transformation of 'Walking on the Spot' from the frantic and unconvincing song that Crowded House had demoed in their earliest days, to the doleful lament it became. And it was Hart, under Finn's instruction, who wrote the brass parts for 'Together Alone'.

Finally, a consideration of *Together Alone*'s key players should acknowledge Seymour's quite audacious album art. Crafted by the bass player as a sculpture in the Los Angeles garage of the producer Tchad Blake, the cover image shows a bright red car, inside of which are three religious figureheads: Jesus, Buddha and another in the backseat hidden behind a curtain, with only their arm visible as it rests on the window. This unseen figure is, of course, Muhammad. Seymour's original version showed Muhammad fully revealed, prompting this image to be shown to a friend of the band, Richard Thompson, a follower of Sufism, who took offence and urged Seymour to reconsider depicting the prophet. This was roughly four years on from the very public fatwa issued to

Salman Rushdie on the back of *The Satanic Verses*. The passage of time has shown altering the artwork to be a wise move (to put it mildly) given global events since the album's release – not least the 2005 cartoon controversy involving Danish publication *Jyllands-Posten* or the mass shooting at *Charlie Hebdo* magazine in Paris in 2012.

Seymour's intention in showing these three characters was to reflect the multiple philosophies and theologies that collided during the band's time at Karekare. Promoting the album on Canadian TV, he said:

> The [idea] came to me at a set of traffic lights in Auckland when I was going into town one time from Karekare Beach … and there were three Samoan gentlemen in a 1964 red Riley going for a drive together, and they were huge guys compacted into this little thing. And I thought to myself, that is when you get your best thinking done, when the three or four people are confined to a car and they get to converse and discuss belief systems on their little journey, which was like the making of our new album *Together Alone*.
>
> (Crowded House Live! 2009)

Seymour was being a bit glib here, but aligning the artwork's concept with the diverse crew of personalities that convened at Karekare confirms his intention to capture the convergence of multiple belief systems under one roof: Youth's paganism, Finn's scepticism, Māori spirituality and myth, and indeed Catholicism. Both Seymour and Finn were brought up in the faith, and during recording, a Catholic wedding took place at the house/studio – the groom being one of the band's helpers – involving a priest who was extremely unimpressed with the whole scene.

The image shows the bundling together of different doctrines, creeds and spiritual identities into one containing vessel, the car, which might represent the corporeal experience of life on earth. The message appears to be that everyone's journey takes a universal path, regardless of which system or faith they follow; despite differences, we are all in the car. The artwork is therefore an attempt to express acceptance, multi-theism, pluralism and inclusivity.

4 Ancient streams: At Karekare

karekare

1. (verb) to be rough (of the sea), choppy, agitated.
2. (noun) surf, waves.

(Te Aka Māori Dictionary)

It is almost dusk and I am walking alone at the southern end of Karekare Beach. Looking north, to my left is Paratahi Island, a darkening jagged shape emerging out of the water. Apparently, when the tide is low, you can walk up to it and touch the rock from the sand, but right now it is formidably cut off by frothing surf. Ahead of me, slightly to the right near the path that goes past the surf club back to the road, is Te Matua (The Watchman), the blade-like dacite monolith that towers over this stretch of beach, and the focal point of much history and legend. Also up ahead is one of the signature sights of Karekare: a large tumbling corridor of sea spray that snakes its way out of the water and across the sand, nearly reaching the base of Te Matua (Figure 4.1).

All around me, the black sand of the shore and dunes provides a powerful ambience. Black sand beaches are not uncommon – especially on New Zealand's North Island. But here, between the rich dark green of the vegetation and the frenetic currents of the sea, it feels especially awesome and encompassing. It is a lengthy walk from the beach's entrance to the waterline – several football pitches' worth when the tide

Figure 4.1 *Sea spray moves across the beach at Karekare. Photo: Barnaby Smith.*

is low – and at certain points, the black engulfs you as if it were a desert, extending on and on in all directions. It is eerie and tense, an almost lunar environment. In some moments, it is as if the blackness is reflected everywhere, the dark sand mirrored in the dark sky. The line from 'In My Command' about a sky the colour of coal comes to mind.

Today, the sand has a particularly velvety tinge due to heavy rain over the last twenty-four hours. The black is of different shades in different places, depending on whether the sand is coloured by the tide or by the rain, making it all the more vivid a sight. Walking along barefoot, churning up the sand, feels a little like trudging through an enormous Black Forest cake. To the northwest, the sun is scheming to break through the low cloud, and it is nearing the end of a day that has veered between merely overcast and periods of horizontal rain and umbrella-inverting wind.

Reminders come a couple of times an hour that this place is not far from the pace and commerce of contemporary life. Just south of Karekare, passenger jets emerge from the western sky on descent to Auckland Airport. Because of this proximity, one can never feel truly untethered from industry and society, along with the knowledge that Karekare is a hub of swimming, surfing, hiking and hang-gliding. These West Auckland beaches are a recreation ground – even if there is not another soul on the beach at this moment.

It is mid-winter, and Karekare Beach is sublime by any standard – the view is like a Caspar David Friedrich painting come to life. But it is no place for bucolic reassurance. It is daunting and haunting. The black sand, the intense green and the grey skies play a part in this, but there is more. 'It's a powerful place,' said Neil Finn in 2013. 'It's not an easy place to be in some ways, there's a lot of energy there and it's quite confronting, but it's a good energy for music' (Interview). And in 2021: 'Karekare was an elemental place that brought out a lot of extreme emotions, both euphoria and desperation I think. Anyone who's been [there] will know that it's a valley of great beauty but it also has an undercurrent, all of which I think you can hear on the record' (Fangradio 2021a).

Varied ambiences

I am coming to the end of a five-day stay at Karekare, dwelling on why I travelled here and what I was looking for. Trying to better understand *Together Alone*? Get closer to it? Feel what the band felt when they were here? Visiting Karekare is something many Crowded House fans from across the world have done; it is undoubtedly a kind of pilgrimage. But I have made pilgrimages before: to many graves of writers and musicians, from James Joyce to Nick Drake to Jack Kerouac, and often come away feeling empty. There is no essence of the person at their grave – it is in their work, just as *Together Alone* can only really be found on the record. So the idea of visiting Karekare as some kind of homage seems dubious. But within five minutes of arrival that feeling dissipates – there is the pulsing essence of so many things here, that go far beyond Crowded House; yet these are things that Crowded House without question incorporated into *Together Alone*.

This Karekare visit became an exercise and experiment in psychogeography: one that is informed by the album, as well as the aspects of Karekare that informed and influenced it. As mentioned in Chapter 2, when first theorized by Guy Debord, psychogeography applied to an urban environment. It was conceived as a politically subversive idea intended to challenge the ideology behind urban planning and the dehumanizing nature of cities designed in the service of capitalism. The essence of the practice was to explore and reinterpret one's surroundings, ideally on foot, according to arbitrary, subjective and perhaps whimsical factors – as opposed to movement through an environment that is impelled by work, profit, duty or necessity. Getting lost is a creative act, one that reshapes and reimagines one's physical participation in the world and sense of place. Though often playful, psychogeography as constructed by Debord was a serious philosophy designed to bring a new, vibrant scope to an individual's relationship with a city. Through a process of proactive defamiliarization, psychogeography resists the city layout's role in supporting economic imperatives.

However, one of the most attractive things about this concept is its malleability and the fact that it can be personalized; it is 'hydra-like' (Billingsley 2017). Today, it goes beyond the metropolitan – indeed, one of the greatest proponents of psychogeography, long before Debord gave it a name, is the Genevan philosopher Jean-Jacques Rousseau, whose countryside wanderings are poeticized in works such as *Reverie of a Solitary Walker* (1782). How can psychogeography be defined as it relates to this visit to Karekare?

It is important to note that psychogeography is 'a practice and not really an academic field' (The Institute of Art and Ideas 2020). So says English writer Will Self, one of the most prominent contemporary practitioners and theorists of psychogeography. It is also worthwhile returning to Debord's original statement:

> Geography, for example, deals with the determinant action of general natural forces, such as soil composition or climatic conditions, on the economic structures of a society, and thus on the corresponding conception that such a society can have of the world. *Psychogeography* could set for itself the study of the precise laws and specific effects of the geographical environment, consciously organized or not, on the emotions and behavior of individuals. The adjective *psychogeographical,* retaining a rather pleasing vagueness, can thus be applied to the findings arrived at by this type of investigation, to their influence on human feelings, and even more generally to any situation or conduct that seems to reflect the same spirit of discovery.
>
> (Debord 1955)

Three aspects of this should be emphasized. First, that psychogeographic thinking can be applied to settings that are 'consciously organized or not', surely leaving ample scope for psychogeographic inquiry in a rural environment. Secondly, Debord refers to the idea's 'pleasing vagueness', which has allowed this concept to stretch and evolve in numerous directions in the nearly seventy years since it emerged, incorporating other disciplines and ideas. And thirdly, a 'spirit of discovery' – central to any venture in psychogeography, including this one at Karekare.

Self's assertion that psychogeography is a practice begs the question of what exactly that entails. The short answer is walking. But walking in a particular frame of mind, informed by the concept of the 'dérive', which translates as 'drift'. Put simply, this is aimless wandering without purpose or much direction. Debord described it as 'a technique of rapid passage through varied ambiances [sic]', adding that '[d]érives involve playful-constructive behavior and awareness of psychogeographical effects, and are thus quite different from the classic notions of journey or stroll' (Debord 1956).

For a more contemporary summary of this idea, and one that I applied at Karekare, Self is helpful. In practising the dérive, he says:

> You abandon your normal preoccupations, you give up trying to work-life balance, and you simply move forward into life, into the environment without some kind of calculation of … a kind of metric formulated by time and money … The dérive is to chuck out that on-board meter we're all suffering from, and instead to … move through the environment with no preconceptions, no destinations. It is the true idea that it's about the journey, not what's at the end of it.
>
> (The Institute of Art and Ideas 2020)

Having been drawn to Karekare by *Together Alone*, I have undertaken a great deal of un-factored, largely purposeless walking without any real consideration of time beyond the day's changing light. After arrival, I had no plan, no itinerary, and no intentions aside from just being here and mapping the place for myself on foot. I retraced my steps and repeated routes over and over to observe sites at different times of day; I also ran particular routes to encounter places in a different physical state. I must have been up and down the beach ten or twelve times in total.

My experience departs from Self's dictum for psychogeography in that I did have certain guiding forces – I always had *Together Alone* in mind whilst walking, mulling over certain lyrics or musical textures in response to the landscape and sometimes following a route suggested by these. I listened to the album while sitting on the beach, and the next day while walking on the beach and cliffs. Finn has said, 'I don't think *Together Alone* makes any more sense ever, to anybody, than when it's played at Karekare' (Neilfinn.com 2016). The notion that music can be understood 'better' in one place over another feels highly questionable, given the subjectivities involved and the personal nature of listening. However, listening to the album here did bring a new feeling to certain tracks: opener 'Kare Kare' above all, with its spectral expression of the place, as well as, interestingly, the song that always felt the most incongruous on *Together Alone*, 'Locked Out'. Never a favourite, listening at Karekare gave the track layers and momentum that were previously hidden.

Another way I may have transgressed from the loosely defined psychogeographic framework is that, for some of the time here, I had company. My guide is Sir Bob Harvey, a man who knows Karekare more deeply than almost anyone. Harvey has been a significant figure in New Zealand public life for over fifty years. After a career in high-level advertising, he was mayor of West Auckland between 1992 and 2010; he has also been highly influential in the Aotearoa cultural sector (particularly film). Mention any New Zealander of world renown, there's a good chance he knows them personally. Sir Edmund Hillary was a close friend.

Harvey's first visit to Karekare came in 1956, and since then, he has been a lifeguard on the beach every season, making him one of the longest-serving lifeguards in New Zealand. He is also an author, and among his books is *Rolling Thunder: A History of Karekare*. He owns a beach house here and has cultivated an intimacy with the entire West Auckland region, and Karekare specifically, that is as couched in wonder as it is formed from the perspective of a historian and politician. On my first visit, he took me to Karekare's most significant sites, many of which are also part of the *Together Alone* story.

The land is moving

The Māori history of Karekare is complex, involving multiple iwi (tribes) and sub-tribes going back over a thousand years. The Tangata Whenua ('people of the land') of the Waitakere Ranges, of which Karekare is part, are the Te Kawerau ā Maki people. This iwi's lineage can be traced to the earliest waka (canoe) migrants (900–1100AD), as well as the prominent historical iwi, the Ngā Oho (1400–1600) (Te Kawerau ā Maki 2023). The Te Kawerau ā Maki are among the older tribes in the Tāmaki Makaurau (Auckland) region, and count as an ancestor of the exalted warrior Tiriwa, said to have uplifted the Rangitoto Island volcano from Karekare Beach and placed it in the Hauraki Gulf, in a show of strength (Taonui 2017). The iwi's name comes from its eponymous ancestor Maki, who settled in northern sections of Tāmaki Makaurau in the seventeenth century (Te Kawerau ā Maki n.d.).

Over the centuries, the Te Kawerau ā Maki lived on the ocean's bounty (shellfish in particular) and cultivated kumara (sweet potato) in the fertile Waitakere soil. Clashes with other tribes were common: 'In those days [the seventeenth and eighteenth centuries], peace was hard to come by, and at Karekare horrific and bloody battles were fought,' writes Harvey in *Rolling Thunder* (2001: 34).

In the 1820s, violence came to Karekare on a scale that would irrevocably affect the Te Kawerau ā Maki, inflicting trauma that would seep into the landscape itself. Between 1820 and 1845, up to 200,000 people were killed in Aotearoa's so-called 'Musket Wars', in which Māori tribes armed with the weapon (procured by trading with settlers) wrought havoc against those that were not, over 'major transgressions and minor insults' (Harvey 2001: 36). A slaughter of the Te Kawerau ā Maki occurred at Karekare in 1825, at the hands of the powerful musket-toting Ngāpuhi tribe. One of the terrible episodes in this tragedy occurred at Te Matua, and it is to the base of this looming rock formation that I am brought first by Harvey.

He shows me a large mound, just past the surf club as you walk towards the beach from the road, and says it is a sacred grave site full of human bones. The climax of this slaughter saw the final smattering of Te Kawerau ā Maki warriors driven to the top of Te Matua by their attackers, where they had no choice but to jump voluntarily to their deaths (it is a fifty-metre drop) or be shot or thrown off the rock.

A short walk back to the road and up a small incline, and Harvey points out the site of another atrocity. Wharengarahi is a magnificent sight as you look up at it, an enormous cave that appears as a great gaping mouth in the side of the valley. During the one-sided battle, Te Kawerau ā Maki women, children and elders hid in this cave as the carnage unfolded. The Ngāpuhi smoked them out using burning manuka brush, forcing them, again, to jump to their deaths or suffocate in the caves. 'Parents, knowing the fate of their children, would have killed them,' writes Harvey. 'Any remaining survivors would have been soon put to death, although strong men and beautiful women were taken as slaves' (Harvey 2001: 37).

After this event, Karekare's name, for a period, changed to 'Mauaharanui', meaning 'place of great wrongdoing'. It is believed that some Te Kawerau ā Maki survived the battle by hiding in caves slightly north at Mercer Bay. What was left of the iwi lived in exile in the Waikato until 1835, after which time they returned to their ancestral lands of the wider Waitakere region (New Zealand Government 2014). They did not, however, return to Karekare due to beliefs around 'tapu', rendering the site of so much death forbidden and sacrosanct. Karekare had been a place of mourning for the Te Kawerau ā Maki for almost two centuries by the time a ceremony was held at the beach in 2003, attended by iwi elders (and Harvey), marking the unveiling of a pou whenua (a carved wooden post to mark a territorial boundary). This event 'signified the return of Te Kawerau ā Maki to Karekare ... the restoration of mana [authority or power] was being acknowledged' (Harvey, n.d.).

Crowded House appear to have had at least some awareness of the violence and displacement in Karekare's history. Paul Hester said: 'A lot of stuff has gone down in that area of New Zealand, and I think that rubbed off on us. The Māori folklore really made sense and we would dream about it at night' (Bourke 1997: 254). One of Finn's most telling comments after the album was finished also feels resonant in relation to the historic suffering and exile of the Te Kawerau ā Maki: 'Almost every theme on the record was about *loss*' (Bourke 1997: 262).

Across the road from Wharengarahi is the path descending to Karekare Falls, and Harvey points me down. The band swam in the waterhole here during their first days at Karekare, and it is where Finn jumped in and let out an underwater primal scream later in the project (Bourke 1997: 254). It also may be here where Youth buried his crystals (Finn interview 2013). Today, it is almost impossible to stand near the water because the recent rainfall has made the cascade especially powerful and, as on the beach, a thick mist of spray fills the entire rocky scene.

The final place Harvey takes me to is the house at 20 Karekare Road, less than five minutes' walk from the waterfall back towards the beach (Figure 4.2). Nowadays a luxurious holiday rental, there is no one here now. With respectful solemnity, we walk over a small bridge (the original version of which was presumably built for Crowded House), up the steep driveway, and the commanding 'grey bunker' appears before us.

The exterior is largely the same as when the band were here, even if the surroundings are very different. For one thing, the paddocks that were all around the house back then have been subdivided into blocks upon which slick modern houses now sit. For another, the house's gardens, front and back, are dominated by large, privacy-giving trees and shrubs, in contrast to the open land and lawns that appear in the electronic press kit. We have a quick look around the back and spy the pseudo-amphitheatre and the space where throngs of people crammed to record 'Together Alone'. A signpost indicates the Ahu Ahu Track that leads to the beach. The house

Figure 4.2 *20 Karekare Road as it is today. Photo: Camille Sanson.*

is not visible from the road and is a fair distance from the nearest neighbour – a distance that would have been much greater in 1992. Nevertheless, a man I bump into another day remembers Crowded House's time here: 'It was very hard for me. I live just below there, and the drummer used to start playing every day at 9 a.m.'

Returning to the road, we are confronted by a sight that makes a dérive at Karekare at this time a bittersweet activity. On the eastern side of the road, three large houses have slipped down the hillside – they are nigh on obliterated; it is grimly spectacular. Through a window, I can see furniture such as beds and tables bunched together at catawampus angles. This, and many similarly destroyed properties in the area, is the result of Cyclone Gabrielle, which wrought destruction on the North Island in mid-February 2023 (it is now late July). Major landslips meant that Karekare was completely cut off for a time, with supplies dropped by helicopter.[1] At the time of my visit, those displaced were still in temporary accommodation. Harvey arrived at Karekare the day after Gabrielle hit and has been involved with the recovery, yet he still expresses disbelief while walking with me five months after the event. He is also attuned to the more subtle changes in the landscape caused by the cyclone – he points out a new slip on a hillside in the distance. 'The land is moving,' he says. Harvey also suggests that the weather event removed layers of earth at Karekare to reveal 'ancient streams' and waterways that have begun flowing once again.

On one of my many walks without Harvey, I return to the base of Te Matua. This time, I walk around its westernmost point that faces the ocean and turn north, and immediately come upon another, much smaller rock in the sand. This is Te Tokapiri, also known as Tom Thumb Rock. This rock is part of a central Te Kawerau ā Maki legend about the greater rock, Te Matua. The story is that during the age of Te Ao Kohatu (the Māori ancient world), Te Matua fathered two children. The pair would play together on the beach until one became disobedient and ventured too far. When the Te Ao Kohatu ended, this unruly child was frozen in place away from his parent and became Paratahi Island. The more pliant child

---

[1] 'The severity and the damage that we are seeing has not been experienced in a generation,' said then New Zealand prime minister Chris Hipkins at the time (McClure 2023). In a message to his mailing list in February 2023, Finn wrote, 'We feel fortunate to have escaped the worst of the effects here at Roundhead Studios, but have been hearing all week of friends and neighbors who were not so lucky with landslides, flooding and isolation leaving many without homes, and some without loved ones.'

became Te Tokapiri and remains a stone's throw from Te Matua on the beach. Here is another example of loss as an abiding theme in a key Karekare narrative.

No other language

Together Alone and *The Piano* are the most high-profile of Karekare's pop culture associations. Many visual artists have captured this landscape too.[2] But there is another artistic treatment of Karekare, a literary one, that is especially resonant when attempting to understand this intricate and unpredictable place. This comes from the New Zealand poet Allen Curnow (1911–2001), a one-time Karekare resident. Several of his poems might stand as their own psychogeographic reading of the locality, as well as bringing a rich interrogation of the nature of perception and the psychology of place, acting as an intellectually inquisitive counterpoint to the intoxicating reverie of *Together Alone*.

Three Curnow works are on my reading list at Karekare: 'Another Weekend at the Beach', 'The Loop in Lone Kauri Road' and 'Lone Kauri Road'. In the first of these, the speaker gives the reader directions to the beach:

> Turn left at the sign: Lone Kauri Road
> winds down to the coast. That's a drop
> of about five hundred feet. Look out
> for the waterfall, the wooden bridge,
> the mown grass, the pohutukawa glade.

---

[2] Notable New Zealand painters to produce works depicting Karekare include William Menzies Gibb, Frank Wright, Stanley Palmer, Gretchen Albrecht and Richard McWhannell.

> The western horizon will have slid
> behind the mask of an eye-levelled
> next eyeballing wave. Park here. Proceed
> on foot …

(1997: 10–11)

Here, Curnow positions the reader in 'three-dimensional space' (O'Brien 2018) and offers them the chance to form their own impressions and find their own way, as opposed to a more closed subjective-emotional reading of the landscape. The language of this poem has a flavour of tourism to it, and an unceremonious directness – the directions may be for someone trying to reach the Karekare Beach beauty spot. The title, 'Another Weekend at the Beach', for one critic, 'has an immediately trivialising effect', while the poem is a 'world of signs' (Arvidson 1997). The poem illuminates the tension between Karekare as a pleasant destination for daytrippers and recreation, and as a place to acknowledge the unknowable and inexpressible ways of nature. Karekare as a place for backpackers in a rented campervan to lunch, versus Karekare as rendered on *Together Alone*. Away from the road and civilization, signs and language end: later in the poem, apparently at the beach, the speaker admits to having '… found no word / or forgot or omitted to write / it down …' The distinctions made by Curnow here are useful while walking and re-walking at Karekare.

'The Loop in Lone Kauri Road' offers different insights. Again, we are at Karekare – on foot and, it seems, in Curnow's mind as he provides a more spontaneous, personal and stream-of-consciousness account. This poem might be interpreted more straightforwardly as an exercise in psychogeography and a kind of dérive, but if we are to regard it as such, we can see that the poet has a wry, gently mocking attitude towards the practice. The poem opens with a sense of weary indecision about what mindset to adopt on this walk:

> By the same road to the same
> sea, in the same two minds,
> to run the last mile blind or
> save it for later. These
> are not alternatives.

The poem then laments: 'So difficult to concentrate!' (a beseeching that returns in the final stanza – 'Concentrate!') before these telling lines arrive:

> A studied performance, the way
> I direct my eyes, position
> my head, 'look interested'.

(1997: 56–7)

It is as if the poet senses the pressure to 'feel something' as they wander this supposed coastal idyll, to achieve some profound enlightenment in response to the surroundings. To further mock the idea of observation as some kind of meditative (or sacred) act, the poem then introduces a dog that 'places a healthy turd' – the poet and the dog's owner then 'like it in the sun'. 'The Loop in Lone Kauri Road' also has Curnow crossing paths with someone out for a jog, and in a piece of pleasing serendipity – the kind that seems to be common in Karekare connections and interactions – it turns out this runner Curnow encounters is none other than Sir Bob Harvey, preparing for a marathon in the mid-1980s: 'NEW YORK STATE jogs past me, / ribcage under the t-shirt / stacked with software … '.

'Lone Kauri Road' is something else again. This poem appears to question the capacity of language and art to respond to, or express, the natural world (a common idea in Curnow's work).

As the poet attempts to survey the seascape and terrain, three times in this poem the line appears: 'Everything was backing away' – the world recoils from being captured or contained in poetry. Elsewhere, Curnow observes 'the sea / with one voice only, its own, / spoke no other language than that one' (1997: 155–6). The poem is a reflection on the relationship between perception and language, and things; and the often extravagant projection involved when human beings respond to what is put before us in the universe.

Besides the Karekare connection, Curnow's poetry does not have a great deal in common with *Together Alone*. This makes it a useful, steadying counterpoint when attempting a psychogeographic practice here. It is easy to get carried away visiting Karekare as a Crowded House fan. The album itself is such a concoction of heightened emotions, metaphysical ideas and melodic beauty; combined with the imposing landscape and spiritual resonance of the place, it can be quite overwhelming to spend concentrated time here. Curnow's poems have a grounding effect to prevent one from becoming too drunk on the place and the music; to avoid being 'up in the stars somewhere', as Mark Hart described Youth (one critic described Curnow as having 'not a flicker of sentimentality' [O'Sullivan 2018]). Along with a sturdy umbrella, some Curnow poems are a good addition to one's kit when visiting Karekare and are intriguing companion texts to *Together Alone* when experiencing the environment and 'energy' here. His poetry is a bit like those planes that fly past at regular intervals – reminders of the logical and social world. His work, particularly 'Lone Kauri Road', offers some crossover with John Ruskin's idea of the pathetic fallacy – that is, the assigning of human traits and qualities to the non-human world (the sea, the beach, the valley), and the risk of 'emotional falseness' that arises from that.

(Possible examples of the pathetic fallacy on *Together Alone*, incidentally, come in 'Fingers of Love', in which the waves take on a sentiment of joy, and 'Private Universe', which implores the summer to remove a curse.)

Suspend disbelief

All this said, it is very difficult not to be transported by Karekare, especially when experienced together with the album, and I failed to remain particularly objective or maintain the detachment of a Curnow poem. Such things are challenging in the company of Harvey, whose attachment to Karekare verges on the devout. Harvey is a pragmatist whose success in business and politics does not suggest someone prone to new-age-infused ideas about spirituality. Yet he talks about Karekare with the ardent devotion of a zealot. 'The place exudes energy, I think, magical energy,' he says. He believes that here one can 'talk to the landscape', adding that it's a place of 'truth' and 'revelation'. When faced with an obstacle in professional or personal life, he has come and slept on the beach, and woken with answers and resolve. 'Something is there,' he says, 'and it's not evil or spooky or creepy, it's a kind of openness. It opens your heart, and it opens you' (Interview 2023). In *Rolling Thunder*, he states Karekare is a place to 'suspend disbelief', that 'allow[s] you to believe in other worlds' (2001: 17).

All this is in my head when I undertake a long clifftop walk along Comans Track north towards Mercer Bay. During this hike, I sat down to make the following (only very slightly edited) notes. It feels appropriate to present this here as a quote, to establish a certain distance from it, as in that moment I was in a heady bubble of something approaching euphoria – or was it 'emotional falseness' – informed by the surroundings and having listened to *Together Alone* shortly beforehand.

> A place you have to meet both emotionally and physically, as if it has laid down a challenge, or asked a question, and it is your proactive duty to respond. You have to meet it halfway, and bring yourself to read it. Karekare has expectations of you. It is as if you and the landscape are lifting something heavy together and it requires your combined strength to do so. Have to meet it, match it, there is a pressure on you to do that. What is the result? Some kind of connection, communion, self-realisation? Not really; unlike other environments I have been moved by, I don't feel I will leave Karekare a changed person. It doesn't let you take it with you. Your bond with the place exists here and here alone. You have to come to it: it is a difficult place to carry in memory and turn to for emotional sustenance. The weight that you and the land lift together is too heavy to leave with. The character of the place is standoffish, uncompromising, firm.

Taking everything into account – the feelings and impressions left by the album, the Māori history and myth, Sir Bob Harvey, Curnow's poetry, and the sheer topography – it is these kinds of thoughts that ultimately win out, even if they might seem extravagant and indulgent in retrospect. Based on what Finn and others have said about their time at Karekare, with its undercurrents and sense of something 'confronting', and the lyrical themes of the songs, the band felt this 'weight' too and met the 'challenge' laid down by the landscape.

While walking the cliffs on this sunny day, I was fortunate to witness a weather phenomenon that several people have described experiencing at Karekare. 'There were days when you'd be looking out and there'd be this mist rolling in from the sea,' said Hester, 'and it would change the valley, it would go from sunny to dark and misty' (Green 2016a). Finn recalled something similar (Interview 2013), and Harvey spoke about this too. A few hundred metres offshore, a large cloud of mist and spray gathered itself directly on the surface of the water against the bright blue sky (Figure 4.2). It was about the size of a large sports stadium, and appeared to expand as it moved closer to land. Within half an hour, it had enshrouded the cliffs, and Karekare had become a different place. It was suddenly like walking in a large-scale piece of immersive art, with the senses suddenly stimulated to sharp sensitivity. It is easy to see how a song's (and a person's) mood would transform amid this. 'Everything was backing away' goes the Curnow line – in this moment, it felt like the exact opposite.

Figure 4.3 *Mist rolling in just north of Karekare Beach. Photo: Barnaby Smith.*

5 Abstract thought: Song by song

The songs of Neil Finn resist straightforward interpretation. Replete with symbolic imagery, his lyrics are famously ambiguous and inconclusive. Rather than relying on any unfolding narrative or linear sequence, his style is to present suggestive associations of ideas, statements and images. You would not describe Finn as a storyteller.

There are few clear-cut emotional positions in Crowded House songs. A sense of place or setting is often muddled, distorted or oneiric, and the voices (and inner voices) of multiple characters can be expressed in a single song. Finn's lyrics often evoke the fuggy disassociation of memories or stream-of-consciousness thought. A resolve to approach lyric writing this way emerged around the time of *Temple of Low Men*, partly to shake off Lennon-McCartney comparisons.[1] Chris Bourke in *Something So Strong* writes: 'From now on … he would be less concerned about having lines make literal sense, than the sounds of words and the strength of their individual images' (Bourke 1997: 124).

Granted, there are numerous exceptions to this in the Crowded House/Finn oeuvre. Songs with an unequivocal meaning include 'Into Temptation', 'Chocolate Cake', 'She Goes

---

[1] There is a certain irony to the fact that another artist known for a random and experimental approach to lyric writing is indeed John Lennon, with his nonsense poetry and absurdism.

On'; later tracks such as 'Anytime' (solo Finn) and 'Silent House'; and later still 'Recluse' (solo). Songs with well-known origin stories, investing them with meaning, include 'Mean to Me' and 'Hole in the River'. But even some of Crowded House's most famous songs toy with obscurity and surrealism – 'Don't Dream It's Over' with its paper cups and holes in the roof, and 'Weather With You' with its boat on the mantelpiece and the Roman Empire's stoush with blue skies.

This symbolist, cryptic and sketch-like lyrical style reached a peak on *Together Alone*. There is a hallucinatory quality to these songs. Yet, on each track, a discernible, if opaque, thread emerges from the sometimes aleatory mixture of images and declarations. Comments made by Finn about his approach to songwriting, during a talk he gave at Yale School of Medicine in 2012, are germane to *Together Alone*. He describes the early stages of song and lyric composition as a process of 'sound making': 'I'll just start with consonants that rub in a nice way and vowels that vibrate in a good way, and a word will pop out and that will seem to have resonance, and a phrase will appear, and suddenly I'm feeling some emotional weight.' He added:

> I like to keep the subconscious in play as much as possible – the more I can get lyrically without thinking about it, without analyzing it, is better for me. I'm happy to write abstract thought after abstract thought that just fell out of my mouth … They are usually really good – they don't make sense necessarily but there's threads that you can get in them.
>
> (Yale School of Medicine 2017)

The songs on *Together Alone* are examples of these 'threads' emerging amid abstraction, and this track-by-track chapter will attempt to identify some of them.

These readings of the thirteen songs should be prefaced by a qualifying statement. Finn has stated on several occasions that he is disinclined to deconstruct or decode his own lyrics. That is to his credit: it is a fruitless and reductive task to ask any artist to hold audiences' hands through their work. However, this does not stop listeners from interpreting songs, identifying meaning, allusions and symbols according to whatever frameworks or context might be available – indeed, this is intrinsic to being a fan. Furthermore, the fact that Finn's music provokes expansive consideration is proof of its depth. It is when we *do not* feel compelled to conjecture and theorize over songs that there may be a lack of substance.

Therefore, this song analysis considers a range of angles, none of which are conclusive, suggesting ideas and insights for the listening experience. Over the years, Finn has spoken about what certain tracks might represent – certainly how some came into being – and this is illuminating. But the album is such a panorama of imagery, with an emotional tenor that ebbs and flows at differing intensities, that it can draw many valid responses. Any interpretation of the album is a changeable thing that evolves and shifts over a lifetime of listening.

'Kare Kare'

Together Alone's opener is the album's only song that openly responds to the place in which it was recorded. As stated, the track grew out of a jam, urged on by Youth, and is credited to the whole band. From its woozy and exciting opening bars onwards, this is, with due respect to 'I Feel Possessed' from

Temple of Low Men and 'Only Talking Sense' from *Finn*, the most captivating track one Finn has conjured.

'Kare Kare' appears to address Karekare in two clear ways: one, its violent history and two, the band's own experiences there. The song's opening lines, to anyone with knowledge of Te Kawerau ā Maki history, are soberingly vivid. Finn sings of dropping from a wave and of lying in a cave. Te Matua, wave-like in shape, is where Te Kawerau ā Maki warriors 'dropped' to their deaths in 1825. And the cave, Wharengarahi, is where many of the tribe perished while hiding from the Ngāpuhi.

The second verse features various domestic scenes. The mention of a Persian rug, and the dust thereon, references an argument between the band and Youth over keeping things tidy in Nigel Horrocks's house (Bourke 1997: 249). The line about getting the washing done reflects the band's day-to-day needs during the Karekare residency. Two other lines allude to running to escape something – surely an acknowledgement that Karekare is as confronting and intimidating as it is beautiful.

Musically, 'Kare Kare' is simple, economical and direct. The plangent four-note sequence played as the song begins, by Mark Hart on lap steel (0:00–0:16), is dappled over a minor-to-major chord sequence of E minor–C major 7–G major,[2] before Hester's drums cascade into the song. The resonating, eerie tone of these chiming notes (which, because of the ringing lap steel, are mildly evocative of Hawaiian music – further locating us in the Polynesian Triangle) straightaway establishes Crowded House's fourth album as worlds away from *Woodface*.

---

[2] Chords mentioned are mostly taken from the official sheet music for *Together Alone* (piano/vocal/guitar), while acknowledging that the chords on the recordings may be variations on these.

The aforementioned chord sequence contains a suggestion of what is termed in music theory as a 'plagal cadence' (here C major 7 to G major), also known as the 'amen cadence'.[3] This is a simple two-chord progression at the end of a musical phrase often used to sing the word 'amen' to conclude hymns. 'Kare Kare' is far from a hymn, but it does retain a hint of religious or spiritual music, and Hart's opening guitar notes do suggest church bells.

The song's outro (2:40–3:23), with Hester's rampant drumming, is another definitive component of the track as it introduces the album as more expansive and more serious than *Woodface*. During this cacophony, Hart's lap steel rises and falls while Finn is caught up in a vocal tendency that reappears several times on *Together Alone*. This is his improvised, only partly intelligible, slightly off-mic, urgent poetry delivered as songs approach their close. Finn described this habit as 'rants that are usually buried in the midst of band tracks … I do them on a few songs, just kind of stream-of-consciousness to some degree. Sometimes I go back in and try and fashion words out of the noises I was making. But strangely enjoyable to sing after all these years' (Fangradio 2021b). This habit appeared on several *Woodface* tracks (in a fashion most similar to 'Kare Kare' on 'As Sure as I Am'). On 'Kare Kare' it is difficult to decipher Finn's heightened rambling, lending the song additional gravitas and mystique. This psychedelic crescendo subsides with tranquil 'aaahs', the lap steel settles and we are left with a sprawling, fading, ambient synthesizer sound (possibly a Youth contrivance) that could be likened to the soft encroaching of a wave that has broken on a beach.

---

[3] In technical terms, a plagal cadence is when the subdominant chord (IV) leads to the tonic chord (I). In 'Kare Kare' this plagal cadence lands in the relative major of E minor, G major.

A final note on 'Kare Kare' pertains to the quirk of its title: 'Kare Kare' rather than 'Karekare'. It is tempting to see this as intentional: one of several meanings of 'kare' in Māori is 'ripple' – as opposed to the 'rough seas' of 'karekare'. 'Ripple ripple' would be a not-inappropriate play on words for this oceanic setting with its waterfall and streams. But the album credits state that *Together Alone* was recorded at 'Kare Kare Beach', suggesting it is likely a small error that went uncorrected. Consider it Crowded House's *Odessey and Oracle* moment.

'In My Command'

As well as being one of the more underrated works in the Crowded House catalogue, 'In My Command' is among *Together Alone*'s most musically interesting and multifaceted songs.

Opening with aggressively repeated piano chords, fortified by scratchy electric guitar notes, this is a jolt after the serene conclusion to 'Kare Kare'. As the first verse enters, Finn's vocal melody exhibits a tritone (the move from C to G♭ on 'We're standing' in the first verse, 0:08–0:09), which the underlying guitar and bass follow.[4] This has a dissonant effect, which, alongside the song's pace and the rasp in Finn's straining voice, establishes an immediate urgency and restlessness. This is an unsettled track. At this point, the song has a flavour of post-punk or alt-rock, before the franticness is alleviated to something calmer with the final chord of each verse: a held F minor 7. This move to a more harmonious texture is

---

[4] A tritone is sometimes known as the 'devil's interval', and is often a feature of music in horror films.

reinforced in the chorus, where the vocals feel almost like call and response, with Nick Seymour's busy descending walking bass line underpinning yet also countering a sense of rising pressure and anticipation.

The chorus returns as the song progresses, embellished more and more each time by backing vocals – initially just the band's harmonies, but in the final chorus, the Te Waka Huia Cultural Group Choir provides 'aaahs' that climb up the scale to reach a cathartic climax (2:49–2:50). In this exercise in delayed harmonic gratification, a great sense of 'opening up' and reaching a tonal 'home' is achieved. As a result, 'In My Command' achieves a compelling dynamism. A further surprise comes with the bridge, in which Finn hollers lines about a 'holy visitation', before the track concludes with another sequence of instrumental abandon and a tiny smattering of Finn's signature mumbling.

Though ambiguous and open to a wide range of interpretations (even for Finn), 'In My Command' introduces an important theme of *Together Alone*: that of subjugation, dominance and control between individuals. Later tracks, such as 'Catherine Wheels', hint at deviance and darkness in tackling this motif, but here it feels like a slightly more arch, even flippant, treatment. The viewpoint of the song appears to be from one who is merely fantasizing about holding power over another, and this wish is conveyed in a slightly mischievous way. The politely phrased chorus declaration, in which the singer shares a longing to 'trouble' their target in their 'time of need', suggests an invasion of another's private sphere is an unfulfilled desire. The expression of it being a 'pleasure' to hold someone in command also stands out as a quite formal, almost gentlemanly way of declaring a quasi-sadistic compulsion. We appear to be in the presence of someone discussing sinister things with a civil and charming tongue.

An alternative take on the song – backed up by the first verse lyrics, which present individuals on the brink of being subsumed by a foreboding landscape – is that it addresses humankind's ancient and ongoing mission to tame and control nature, and the ultimate impossibility of doing so. A third reading of 'In My Command' is that it addresses the elusive and slippery 'creative spirit' of the artist, or the muse. In the second part of the first verse (0:25–0:39), Finn implores himself not to miss it when a crucial moment of capricious inspiration arrives, begging it to be submissive. In this interpretation, the 'pleasure' of having one's creative faculties harnessed and directed is then the crux of the chorus.

Elsewhere, some of Finn's verse lyrics are typically abstruse and strange, with lines about diplomats and acrobats, and a possible reference to Salvador Dali in a later verse – a dripping clock – adds further colour to this gripping tour de force.

'Nails in My Feet'

Domestic interiors have been a feature of Crowded House songs since the first album. There are kitchens in 'World Where You Live' and 'Weather With You'; a bedroom in 'Whispers and Moans'; a living room in 'Mansion in the Slums'; and a bathroom in 'Not the Girl You Think You Are', to name a few. The promotional video for 'Don't Dream It's Over' passes from room to room of a house.

From the assertive metaphorical pronouncement of its first line on, the song hangs the bulk of its lyrical framework on the layout of a house. 'Nails in My Feet' employs the house as an existential symbol of personhood, as well as the figurative space where another person enters for the sake of connection and closeness. A guided tour of a home becomes a guided tour of the singer's inner world, and the song's temper becomes one of intimacy and vulnerability as this is exposed and explored by the listener. In moving between 'rooms', the track considers the segmentation of the self and the many compartments of identity – and how achieving meaningful knowledge of another person involves a survey of these multiple rooms.

The lyrics sprawl in other directions too. Finn's cry of surrender towards the song's end fits the album's theme of power and control – from the perspective, it seems, of one who is happy to submit. The final verse, Finn has said, is a reference to the true story of someone he heard of, who, on the evening of his birthday, came home to what he thought was an empty house, promptly disrobed and proceeded to indulge in a session of self-love. He was interrupted when everybody screamed 'surprise' as a party was sprung on him (Crowded House 2021).

The song's title is one of the more loaded in Finn's body of work, with its clear biblical associations. Finn has not rejected the connection, stating his belief that an effective lyric is about 'opening doors, and [letting] people walk in whatever door they wish' (Neilfinn.com 2016). The backstory of the title is, in fact, a little prosaic and refers to sandals he wore to aerate the grass tennis court at his grand Melbourne property, which had nails in their soles that would pierce the earth as he walked around (NeilFinn.com 2016).

Whereas 'Kare Kare' has an expansive feel, having grown out of a jam, and 'In My Command' is a clattering rock song with some unusual musical scaffolding, 'Nails in My Feet' is an example of Finn's gift for a taut and chiselled melody. Reminiscent of a nursery rhyme in its simplicity, the verse melody is an exercise in effortless symmetry – this and 'Distant Sun' are probably the 'catchiest' tunes on *Together Alone*. Seymour's bass plays a leading role – one important moment comes in the second chord of the song, for which he plays a D to invert the B diminished chord (0:03), bringing an instability that returns in each verse. Hart's chromatic and twisted guitar solo (1:21–1:43) adds further allure, while Finn delivers his dreamiest mumble-singing prior to the fade-out.

In challenging dismissals of the band as AOR (adult-oriented rock, which basically means bland), a British critic once said of Crowded House that they are 'AOR in the way The Beatles "For No One" [*sic*] was AOR – bittersweet and capable of leaving an aching hole where your heart used to be' (Bourke 1997: 200). This observation feels particularly applicable to 'Nails in My Feet'.

'Black and White Boy'

Driven by a guitar riff that sounds like a passing bullet, 'Black and White Boy' has been described by Finn as the band's 'tribute to glam rock' (Green 2016a), even if it started as a gentle ballad (comparable with 'Into Temptation' according to Hart [Bourke 1997: 253]). There is a strong swagger in its frenetic rock and roll, and it is one of the more straightforward (though satisfying) tracks on the album.

It also has the album's least ambiguous lyrics. The track is a portrait of someone whose personality is defined by unpredictable extremes: in some moments joyful and charming, at others demonic and malicious. Some fans and critics have assumed Finn had Hester in mind with the song, and the lyrics do correspond with comments Finn made about his friend over the years. In a 1994 interview, he said: 'As much as he's incredibly funny when he's up … the other side of that is very black and it became that we would wake up on any given day and not know whether we would find him up or down. It was quite a burden' (Fyfe 1994, cited in Bourke 1997: 316). Finn has said the song's title was inspired by his Dalmatian, Lester and the affectionate name given to the hound by Finn's friend, the New Zealand poet Sam Hunt (Neilfinn.com 2016).

There is a connection between the subject of this song – the volatility and erratic nature of a certain kind of personality – and the quickly changing meteorological conditions at Karekare, as discussed in Chapter 4. In this place, a sudden shift in weather could occur without warning and transform the mood in an all-encompassing way. 'Black and White Boy' might be seen as a reflection of this, transposed to the individual psyche. If it is indeed about Hester, the song assumes a unique place in the Crowded House catalogue as a contemplation of the character of one of the band's members.

In terms of musical structure, in true garage rock style, 'Black and White Boy' establishes its simple pattern and does not develop or deviate a great deal. It is nevertheless an accomplished and absorbing piece (one can imagine Youth enjoying and encouraging the transition from gentle ballad to loud rocker, and he may have been behind the inventive use of handclaps) that is sandwiched between two slower, more emotive tracks. A particularly stirring passage comes when Hart's heavily played (if low in the mix) power chords amplify the song's bluster as the final bridge concludes (2:57–3:01). Another subtly diverting moment comes when Finn toys with the chords of the chorus, which in this track basically amounts to the one titular line. In these sections, the phrase 'black and white boy' is sung over the song's insistent three-chord riff (B♭ major–C major–D major) each time it arrives, except for one occasion (2:29) when it jumps directly to the D major from the preceding F# major 7 (also the chord Hart crunches with such gusto half a minute later), bypassing the other two chords. This leads to a brief intermission where the song feels temporarily satisfied and at ease, drifting between D major and F# minor 7, before launching back into tension again with the A major of the final bridge (2:45).

'Fingers of Love'

As is his fashion, Finn has been open about the origins of this dramatic song while avoiding offering direction regarding its meaning. Finn wrote 'Fingers of Love' while on holiday in Jamaica in 1991, after observing the 'god rays' of the sun breaking through the clouds during sunset (Neilfinn.com 2016).

It opens with a texture somewhat similar to the intro to 'Kare Kare': strummed acoustic guitar adorned with unhurried and vivid electric guitar notes from Hart that are left to ring out theatrically. Hart's later solo is a revered centrepiece of this track – he came to perform it on twelve-string in a live setting, giving it an even grander scale. But another sequence is just as mesmerizing in the studio version: Hart's stunning work in the song's very short bridge, where his guitar scratches and grinds along underneath Finn's vocals (2:08–2:16), before soaring into the solo.

Another definitive instrumental layer of 'Fingers of Love' is the percussion that enters after the first verse (1:11). The Australian percussionist Geoffrey Hales, whose career has spanned world music, jazz and electronica, is a critical presence here. This is the song's slow-beating pulse, suggestive of the rhythmic movements and sounds of many oars moving in unison on a longboat – perhaps Māori waka in the waters off Karekare. The line about jumping overboard supports this maritime angle. It is also worth noting that 'Fingers of Love' was recorded on a 'rainswept, melancholy' day (Bourke 1997: 253) when Karekare would have been at its bleakest, contributing to its swelling and mournful nature.

Lyrically, 'Fingers of Love' is a curious journey. After the first verse's restrained and rather beautiful poetry – and its suggestion of heightened sensory perception with the mention of hearing blades of grass in the breeze – the lyrics take an odd turn towards something a little purple. The extravagant lines about sleeping mad dogs and fallen angels walking on water jump out of the song – and indeed the album – as moments of exaggerated, unexpected and quite melodramatic grandiloquence. This aside, 'Fingers of Love' appears to address once again humanity's smallness amid the uncontrollable and unknowable vastness of nature, and the release to be found in surrendering oneself to this overwhelm. Finn 'won't be helped' and implores the listener to jump overboard. Finn has acknowledged the potential reading of the song's title as sexual – and while welcoming a diversity of angles, he notes its genesis was 'not a particularly sexy moment' (Neilfinn.com 2016).

'Pineapple Head'

First, the time signature: 'Pineapple Head' has a distinctive metre. It is subject to interpretation, but the song may be in 12/8 or 6/8[5] or even a quick 3/4. This format is relatively unusual in pop; songs with a similar time signature include David Bowie's 'Five Years', Wings' 'Let Me Roll It' and Lou Reed's 'Perfect Day'. A 6/8 time is also often associated with jigs, and 'Pineapple Head' does have a mildly Celtic feel (many sea shanties are also in 6/8). Another 6/8 example is 'Norwegian Wood' by The Beatles, and the two songs also share a leaping, buoyant motif (played on acoustic twelve-string here, and George Harrison's sitar in the other).

Interestingly, for a song with such a particular, lively rhythmic pattern, it features only minimal percussion, with Finn's precision-perfect rhythm guitar playing a key role in holding time. Along with Seymour's vibrantly circuitous bass line and Hart's mandolin (possibly a nod to the folky inflection), another important instrumental layer is what is likely a MusicMaster 600 Chamberlin (an early tape replay instrument that predates the Mellotron) using the flute sample,[6] giving further Beatles overtones. This rare piece of gear had previously been used liberally on both *Temple of Low Men* and *Woodface*.

This track also has a well-known lyrical backstory. Finn's young son, Liam, had been suffering from a bad fever, during which he started 'spouting these great lines' (Neilfinn.com 2016), which Finn duly appropriated. As a result, 'Pineapple Head' is, even for him, an especially whimsical and arbitrary series of images. But unlike 'Fingers of Love', nothing feels too earnest in this linguistic frolic – 'Pineapple Head' is one

---

[5] These time signatures have a compound metre, where each strong beat of the bar is grouped in three equal parts, rather than the two of simple metres.

[6] No Chamberlin is mentioned in the album credits, but experts have identified the use of one on 'Pineapple Head' (Thompson n.d.). Eddie Rayner is credited with keyboards.

of Finn's most charming songs. Its lyrical effect comes from the fact that amid the delirium-inspired imaginings, certain direct and accessible lines cut through the abstraction and anchor the song in an emotional register, with a suggestion of narrative. For example, the extremely Lennon-esque line about having known a female friend 'a long time ago' is a moment of relatability and focus, suggesting a point in time, a relationship, a perspective, memory and character. This single line stabilizes the song and develops it from the babblings of a child's fever dream into something more layered. Meaning can also be read into the strange imagery within the context of this departure point. The injection of piercing clarity amid obscurity is among Finn's most effective lyrical devices – this being far from the only example.

'Locked Out'

Like 'Black and White Boy', 'Locked Out' was originally written as a slow ballad, only to morph into a frenetic rocker during the Karekare sessions. At a performance at London's Fleadh festival in 1994, Finn expressed regret at increasing the tempo, remarking that the slower version was a 'better song' (Neil Finn 2012). It was Hart who proposed it be played 'like the Ramones' as Bourke put it; Hart subsequently stated, 'I don't remind [Finn] that it was my idea' (Bourke 1997: 253). A version titled 'Locked Out – Zen Mix' appeared on the 2016 Deluxe edition of the album and shows Finn's initial intention for the song – a hazy, meandering affair – as does a snippet performed at Fleadh.

'Locked Out' is a lean slice of power-pop, and while it would be unfair to call it one-dimensional, it does not quite provide the lyrical or melodic depth of the rest of the album.

However, this simplicity aids *Together Alone*'s balance and pacing; this noisy mid-album track, the third of four loud, high-octane songs, is a suitable dose of energy between the relative oddness of 'Pineapple Head' and the soundscape of 'Private Universe'.

Finn's reasons for transforming the song are not completely clear, but there may have been commercial thinking behind it. The album was taking experimental turns, with many new and strange ingredients drawn from Youth's sensibilities and the group's wish to expand their sound, leading them away from the expectations of both their record label and some fans. Here was a chance to include a song that was bouncy, propulsive, radio-friendly, even danceable. 'Locked Out' would also bring a blast of out-and-out rock and roll to the Crowded House live set that had not really been in their arsenal prior to *Together Alone*. On stage, the band often tagged on exciting instrumental passages to the track's ending, and Hester was afforded further opportunity to 'freak out' and bash away with abandon.

Finn has said the song was inspired by Peter Carey's 1981 novel *Bliss*, and most of the lyrics take a cue from that (Neilfinn.com n.d. c) – including the 'twin valleys' in the sun, though this may also be a Karekare reference. The song touches on *Together Alone*'s themes of possession, control and alienation, while religious imagery returns with the mention of an altarpiece.

The track's structure and chord choices hardly represent Finn at his most innovative or melodious. There is one intriguing moment, though, when 'Locked Out' moves to what just about constitutes a middle eight (1:38–1:52). The vocal melody here, in contrast to the belted-out verses in the middle-upper range of Finn's tenor, lowers and deepens as it hovers on and around

G#3. The significant echo on Finn's voice combines with Hart's also echo-y electric guitar line to produce a darkly psychedelic interlude.

While at Karekare, Finn developed a case of giardia (an intestinal infection caused by a parasite) that he likely contracted by drinking contaminated water. His weight dropped to less than sixty kilograms, and it is an impressive feat of resilience that he continued recording. One wonders, though, how this affected his performance (if at all) – and 'Locked Out' is one track where his voice is noticeably thin and a little nasal, possibly because of his health issues. As it happens, it suits the song well, the straining quality serving both the energy of the arrangement and the hunger of the lyric.

'Private Universe'

The actor Paul Dano, who played Brian Wilson in the biopic *Love & Mercy* (2014), has an interesting take on the Beach Boys song 'God Only Knows', based on an obsessive immersion in Wilson's music for research. Dano believes the song is not directed at a beloved romantic figure; rather, Wilson is addressing music itself, without which his life would be empty (*WTF with Marc Maron* 2016). Correspondingly, here is a theory about 'Private Universe': it is about the creative process; the private universe is the mental and physical space one cultivates for concocting art.

In the Yale talk, Finn details the ritual and care behind creating space and time to compose music. He prioritizes solitude, privacy, order and focus, as well as experimentation, risk and embracing 'unknown pathways' (the title of the lecture). It is a highly personal 'dreamy state' he enters, with an air of the sacred to it. One interpretation of 'Private Universe' is as a paean to this cloistered sphere.

Certain lyrics can be read in a way to support this: the first line's dismissal of discussing the weather suggests a call to more urgent, important matters, while the 'promise' and then 'labour' of love hint at the reward as well as the hard work of creativity. There are lines that propose an objective (1:38–1:41); lines in the second verse that address practice, process and the concept of the muse represented by the birds (1:42–1:57); and a bridge that offers reflection and satisfaction upon completion (2:25–2:50). The short third verse touches on endurance and sacrifice (3:06–3:17). The apple tree is a reference to Finn's secret secluded place during childhood (Bourke 1997: 5). The song was even written in a private universe of sorts: Finn's Melbourne home had a turret in its roof, a small room or 'little sanctuary on top of the house' that he used for writing and demoing (Neil Finn 2018).

There is some crossover, too, with the reading of 'In My Command' as a reflection on catching and controlling the muse: if the earlier track is about taking full advantage when the moment comes, 'Private Universe' is about fostering the right conditions for inviting the creative spark.

Sonically, this is one of the most fascinating Crowded House tracks. First, there is the striking collage of sounds that begins the song. It sounds like a mixture of traffic noises, voices, wind and water, creating a floating ambience that is interrupted by a tabla (played by Noel Crombie, and potentially another Youthism) and the song's central, insistent acoustic chord sequence: A minor–D minor 7/A–A minor 11–A minor. As these chords suggest, the song exists in a small harmonic range, with Finn's vocal melody moving to, from and around a single note (E3), in a way similar to 'Kare Kare'. It is indeed a tight squeeze, as the third verse has it.

The Cook Islands log drummers make their first appearance on the album on this eighth track, delivering an explicit nod to Pasifika music and rhythms. Hart's lap steel, which switches between a crunchy tone on one hand and wailing on the other, has a central role in the busy climax, alongside chirrups of guitar, what sounds like a distorted mandolin, and other oddities.

'Private Universe' took the reverse journey to 'Locked Out' and 'Black and White Boy': it began as a perky, upbeat piece[7] before it was brought under control to become a smouldering, layered experiment. The minimalist version that appeared on *Afterglow* offers a mesmerizing alternative arrangement stripped of its textures, and to this day, whenever Finn performs it solo on acoustic guitar, he brings a more plaintive, even confessional dimension to a song he has often cited as a favourite.

'Walking on the Spot'

The album's shortest track, 'Walking on the Spot', is three minutes of exquisitely formed melodic balladry, sorrowful chord changes, tantalizingly suggestive lyrics and affecting harmonies. First demoed in 1985 (when Finn, Hester, Seymour and guitarist Craig Hooper were known as The Mullanes), its original version was an oddly clumsy pop song with a buoyant tempo and production that overwhelmed the nuance and

---

[7] Included on the 2016 Deluxe version of *Together Alone*.

beauty of its structure.[8] It took shape at Karekare when Finn started playing around with it at the piano one evening. Youth was not present at this moment of transformation, and the producer was reportedly upset that such progress had been made in his absence (Bourke 1997: 255).

Though nothing particularly challenging or unusual, the song's verse chords produce a deep, melancholy effect: D major–B minor–B♭ major–F major. A C6 to transition to the chorus brings suspense and uncertainty, before a seductive change from D minor 7 to D6 (0:43–0:45) is another lovely turn in the melodic circuit. Finn flirts with the upper region of his vocal range, and once again the straining quality amplifies the strength of feeling, as do the understated but integral vocal harmonies. Instrumentally, 'Walking on the Spot' is a relative oddity on *Together Alone*. The only piano-based song, it also features an accordion (played by a friend of the band, Melbourne nightclub owner Dror Erez) and a melodica (played by Seymour).[9] Lap steel provides accents here and there, while a nylon-string guitar is also present (most beautiful at 2:11–2:14).

Lyrically, domestic interiors, scenes and furniture reappear, alongside reflections on infidelity, guilt and existential disorientation. The song's undoubted centrepiece line – 'Can we look the milkman in the eye?' – could be a proverbial saying from post-war Britain and is a powerful, compact, and even witty encapsulation of regret in the wake of submitting to desire. If 'Into Temptation' is the night before, 'Walking on the Spot' is the morning after. It is also a flawless piece of emotive

---

[8] Included on the Deluxe edition of *Crowded House*.
[9] This is uncredited, but Finn has confirmed the melodica (Fangradio 2021a).

songwriting that is among the finest pieces on the album – and indeed, in Finn's career.

'Distant Sun'

The first single to be taken from *Together Alone*, 'Distant Sun' was released on 20 September 1993, a month before the album. Upon hearing it, fans might have reasonably assumed that the forthcoming LP would be generally similar in tone to *Woodface*: the breezy melody and life-affirming lyrics were treading familiar ground. This is the definition of a 'solid' pop song: sophisticated in melody, arrangement and production; eloquent in lyric; and with a polished vocal performance. The much-loved hit is a pleasant and soothing listen, without having quite the emotional penetration of the song it follows, nor the wildness of the one it precedes. It has remained, though, a staple of Finn's live sets, both with Crowded House and solo.

This was a song that benefitted from outdoor recording, with Finn and Hart setting up on the porch, 'shrouded by cold mist' (Bourke 1997: 253). Another track to combine Finn's acoustic rhythm guitar with Hart's electric (this time twelve-string), it is one of the simpler arrangements on the album, without any passages that approach psychedelia or surprising instrumental choices. A highlight comes when Finn's voice jumps an octave halfway through each verse, upping the energy and serving as a smooth transition into the chorus.

Though its lyrics are typically enigmatic and opaque, 'Distant Sun' seems to present a figure of seniority and experience advising and consoling one who is less exposed to life. Finn has said the famous line about seven worlds colliding, and potentially the song's title, is a reference to the Pleiades star cluster, also known as the Seven Sisters (Neilfinn.com n.d. b); mention of sparks and flames, also in 'Pineapple Head', recurs; and there are possible biblical references to floods and vengeance. Finn's late-song improvised mumble-singing returns on the fade-out.

While it is hard to argue that 'Distant Sun' occupies the same ubiquitous cultural status as 'Don't Dream It's Over' or 'Weather With You', it has become one of Finn's most beloved songs and is probably the 'poppiest' track on *Together Alone*. It is also the closest the album gets to an anthemic, mass-sing-along chorus. Its sequencing on the album, down at number ten, is perhaps surprising for such a catchy piece – but its placement does allow it to act as a bright and positive statement prior to the comparative exercise in calvary that is 'Catherine Wheels'.

'Catherine Wheels'

It is difficult to know where to start with this sprawling and turbulent track, which has a psychological impact that takes *Together Alone* to a different plane. 'Catherine Wheels' is the encapsulation of all the factors that fed into the album: the musical and aesthetic priorities, the Karekare backdrop, the more surreal turn taken by Finn's lyrics, Youth's preoccupation with ambience and indeed personal dynamics. Yet it is also a piece with a long history: its earliest version dates to 1978 when Split Enz demoed it as 'First to Say Gone'. The Finn brothers revisited it as 'Catherine Wheel' in their songwriting collaboration of 1989 (and it was therefore in the mix for *Woodface*[10]), before it came together so sensuously at Karekare.

---

[10] 'Catherine Wheel' is found on the Deluxe version of *Woodface*.

Finn's vocals enter a split second before the opening chord of the song, a B7♭9,[11] setting an instant tone of disquiet and nervousness, which is consolidated by the change to E minor (0:03). In this first half of the song, a temporary sense of settlement and resolution is brought by progressions involving G major and C major in both verse and chorus (0:13–0:17; 0:54–0:57), but it is fleeting, and the energy remains unsettled, perturbed. If 'Catherine Wheels' were to conclude at approximately 2:30, after its conventional verse-chorus-verse-chorus format, we would still be left with a devastating song. But here the arrangement takes flight as the band delivers the album's second passage that grew from a jam.[12] The section that acts as a transition from part one to part two of the song (2:23–3:05) features the Te Waka Huia Cultural Group Choir, as a mantric riff emerges from the mandolin, based around D major and D suspended 2nd, with Seymour's bass part also conspicuous. Part two's vocal melody is simple but emphatic, and a compelling contrast with the strange, groovy interlude (3:53–4:12) that sits on a D7 chord, which splits the two sections of part two and later acts as the song's fade-out, accompanied by gnarly lap steel.

With its ominous lyrical imagery and disjointed narrative, 'Catherine Wheels' is the album's most disturbing or even macabre song. Ideas of morality and love are stretched and distorted to the point where they become destructive forces. Yet throughout, there remains a sad beauty and a bewitching

---

[11] The official sheet music has this chord, but in live versions such as at the Corner Hotel in Melbourne in 1996, available on YouTube, Finn appears to play A minor 6 (Green 2016b).

[12] Finn said the track 'was very convoluted and the entire end of it was just a jam – from about three minutes onwards [that's] just what it was' (Interview 2013).

gothic aspect to the words, which certainly 'vibrate in a nice way,' as Finn put it at Yale. The song portrays a complex, serious and deeply felt psychological scenario, probably between two people – Catherine and the mysterious Sad Claude character (at Fleadh, Finn described it as 'a fantasy about the break-up of a very twisted affair' [Neilfinn.com n.d. a]). The first half of the song includes portents of ill fortune (a bad moon rises); reflections on human mortality, entropy and decay; and what could be read as a psychosexual compulsion and connection between two individuals. The second half takes a bleaker turn: there is a character's death here – maybe self-inflicted, maybe at another's hand. There is the return of the theme of dominance and coercion: the male character has a 'hold' on the female, sings Finn, before referring to the woman as a 'slave'. The song also includes fast-moving switches in narrative perspective: at points early on, there is a first-person account of this 'twisted affair', while at others, particularly in the second half, Finn reverts to an omniscient third-person voice – maybe because Catherine, who we were within the first verse, is indeed 'gone'.

The implication of mental and physical abuse has relevance to the song's title: a Catherine wheel was a brutal instrument of torture and execution used mostly in Europe between classical antiquity and the nineteenth century. It is closely associated with Saint Catherine of Alexandria, who was sentenced to death on the wheel in the fourth century[13] (the Catherine wheel firework is named for her). One might also see a connection with Emily Brontë's *Wuthering Heights*, in

---

[13] Legend has it that the wheel shattered when she touched it, and she was beheaded instead.

which Catherine suffers so egregiously amid circumstances that ensure psychological and emotional despair, and her ghost haunts the novel's tempestuous antihero, Heathcliff. The gothic heart of 'Catherine Wheels' is underscored when considered in this light.

That its lyrics inspire such considerations, along with its beguiling melodic twists, unusual structure, sensitive arrangement and overall mystique, makes this arguably the greatest of all Crowded House songs. It is not often performed and is rarely mentioned in mainstream critical appraisals of the band – though it retains a place in Finn's affections. 'I don't play it very often,' he said, 'mainly due to the fact it's quite tricky to learn, and it's long and sprawling. But I'm very fond of it – it's got a very peculiar lyric, it's inhabited by characters with slightly disturbing undertones' (Interview 2013).

'Skin Feeling'

This Hester composition was written at the same time as his 'Italian Plastic' from *Woodface* – around 1989. The track's muscular arrangement took a cue from U2 (Neilfinn.com n.d. d) and is therefore not a challenging or particularly rewarding listen. Yet, like 'Locked Out', it serves a purpose in the running order – 'Skin Feeling' is relaxed and direct after the intensity of 'Catherine Wheels'. The peculiar 'rapping' from Hart is among the song's notable components, while Hester's lyrics express the joys of having vim and vigour renewed on the cusp of middle age.

Another interesting point about 'Skin Feeling' comes with the line that mentions 'people on TV'. This reference to the broad realm of popular culture and media is notable, as it is the first time anything along these lines has arisen on the album. On the band's previous three records, several songs were inspired by or alluded to topical issues or stories, or notorious people (examples include 'Chocolate Cake', 'Kill Eye', 'Fame Is' and 'Don't Dream It's Over'). Up until this twelfth track on *Together Alone*, there has been almost no acknowledgement of wider culture and society – an indication that Finn was aiming for a lyrical landscape that was more psychological and rooted in the sensual perception of nature and environment, going beyond fashion and zeitgeist. This mention of television does not break the spell, though, and listening to 'Skin Feeling' today provides an enjoyable reminder of Hester's idiosyncratic worldview, his vulnerability and his love of watching TV.

'Together Alone'

The day of recording for the album's title track is one of the great occasions in the history of Crowded House. At Karekare, Finn conceived the idea to 'try and write something to draw in what we saw as a few strands of New Zealand music' (Neilfinn.com 2016): a Māori singing group (Te Waka Huia Cultural Choir), the brass bands that Finn recalled fondly from childhood, and the Cook Islands log drummers. This is Crowded House's most conscious attempt at fusion.

As much a celebration as a recording session, the story of the day has been told in detail elsewhere[14] – but it brought an exuberant and probably tension-releasing end to the

---

[14] *Something So Strong* by Bourke devotes the better part of a chapter to the 'Together Alone' recording.

band's time at Karekare, with 600 people present at one point (an after-party took place at a house nearby). Finn wrote the song and collaborated with Te Waka Huia leader Bub Wehi on lyrics, and Hart composed the brass part under Finn's direction to create the Salvation Army band feel. Youth encouraged Crowded House to take responsibility for mobilizing the disparate sections, so Hester organized and conducted the log drummers, and Finn conducted the choir, who performed outside. It is a marvel of a track, though reflecting twenty years later, Finn spoke of its inherent limitations:

> I'm really fond of the piece of music, and I think it turned out really well, but I don't think we explored the depths of Māori music, and in some ways, it was a 'throw it together, see what happens' kind of thing. But I'm really glad we did it, it was an incredible day … but it was also quite stressful as well – a lot to organize and a lot of people. Whenever you do something like that it's always a good idea when you think about it, but then you realize that it *has* to be good.
>
> (Interview 2013)

The band incorporated Māori and Polynesian music into a Western pop idiom with considerable sensitivity and careful intention – this fact, along with Wehi's key composing role, removes any suggestion of cultural appropriation. Tony Mitchell has described Finn as embodying '[an] expansive sense of situatedness which expresses multiple identities rather than narrow, fixed confinements of the national' (2018: 148). This feels applicable to the mission for 'Together Alone'.

The track has a lilting, lullaby-ish feel thanks to its slow pacing, the simplicity and repetition of its melody, and above all, the fact that Finn delivers his most gentle vocal of the album. A breathtaking introduction sees the song drift for a few seconds on a sadly smiling C major chord; the acoustic guitar, speckles of piano and log drums suggest finally floating on calm waters after the stormier conditions at other points on the album (0:01–0:10). The thirty-voice choir's entrance on the first chorus is a jubilant moment, the vigorous confluence of harmonies adding an overt Polynesian aspect to an archetypal Finn melody. The brass band joins for the second verse, bringing the mood of a sad Christmas carol to the already multifarious mixture. The Māori karanga (ceremonial call) heralds the build to the stirring climax, in which this amalgam of traditions concludes the record on an inclusive and forward-looking note. There is also a satisfying symmetry to the fact that the album begins and ends with songs written at Karekare.

Finn based his lyrics on the Māori Rangi and Papa creation myth for the formation of the universe and people. There are numerous variations and layers to this legend, but in essence, the story is: the sky (Rangi) and earth (Papa) are joined inseparably in darkness; in the small space between their bodies, several gods dwell who desire more space. These gods prise Rangi and Papa apart, forcing Rangi to the sky and Papa to be earthbound, causing heartbreak and anguish for both. While Finn's verses are open to wider interpretation, Wehi's Māori lyrics for the chorus directly invoke Rangi and Papa. This myth becomes the concept behind the album's title: two souls experiencing solitude and loneliness separately, but connected by a spiritual bond that unites them in grief and provides a degree of solace. Many listeners are likely to hear 'Together Alone' without knowing the Rangi and Papa story – and it is still a poignant, moving song if interpreted simply as about separated or bereft lovers.

'Together Alone' and *Together Alone* end with the log drummers, as the brass band continues lightly in the background (3:32–3:55). Another sound that emerges is birdcall (which may be the common myna or the tōrea pango/variable oystercatcher), and this brief final document of Karekare is an appropriate and poetic detail as the album closes.

6 The alchemy is complete: Aftermath

Good history

In the seminal book *Revolution in the Head*, Ian MacDonald proposes that The Beatles' most innovative and creative period begins and ends with two iconic chords: the clanging guitar chord that opens 'A Hard Day's Night', the first track on the 1964 album of the same name, and the almighty piano chord that concludes 'A Day in the Life', the final piece on *Sergeant Pepper's Lonely Heart's Club Band* (1967) (1995: 90).

In extending this idea to Neil Finn, it can be given a lyrical slant: the period of his most inventive and ambitious music is bookended by songs that deal with the West Auckland coastline. 'Kare Kare' from *Together Alone* (1993) is the first, with 'Into the Sunset', the closer on the 2001 solo album *One Nil* (a track that refers to Lion Rock and Marine Parade in Piha), the other. Looking back on *Together Alone* today in the context of Finn's overall career, it is clear that it ushered in a time of adventure and vision: after this album came the lo-fi masterpiece in partnership with brother Tim, *Finn* (1995); the rich and experimental solo album *Try Whistling This* (1998) with its use of loops and electronica; and the eclectic, instrumentally diverse *One Nil*.[1] Collaborating with Youth and embracing new

---

[1] Throw into this, the three new Crowded House tracks included on *Recurring Dream*, with 'Instinct' in particular a step in a different direction.

approaches to the recording process and song textures saw *Together Alone* expand Finn's mind in a way that is probably still felt as he creates music today.

This begs the question of whether, in music released since, Finn and Crowded House have hit upon a tone or song style reminiscent of what was achieved on *Together Alone*. That there are few examples is a testament to the fact that this is a work that could only have been created at that place, at that time, with that team. The three aforementioned albums are distinguished in their own way, but each is a marked contrast to the sound of *Together Alone*. *Finn* and *Try Whistling This* in particular are fully realized and exciting explorations of decidedly different musical terrain from what was produced at Karekare.

Finn decided to reform Crowded House in 2006 as he prepared a solo album in which Nick Seymour was emerging as an important figure. That record became the fifth Crowded House studio LP, *Time On Earth* (2007). Back in collaboration with Seymour and Mark Hart, along with American drummer Matt Sherrod, Finn wanted to 'leave some good history in there instead of that big deathly full stop' (Interview 2013) – a reference, of course, to Paul Hester taking his own life in 2005. As the first Finn release after Hester's death, *Time On Earth* is an album tinged with loss, sadness and even regret. Finn's most intense lyrical work since *Together Alone* is coupled with some typically otherworldly melodic constructions (this is not a widely held opinion, but I, for one, regard *Time On Earth* as the band's second-best album). Overall, *Time On Earth* is not closely similar in spirit to *Together Alone*, nor is it as consistent, but certain standout tracks do approach that graceful, complex melancholy.

Among these is the opener, 'Nobody Wants To', with that familiar emotive and ghostly electric guitar; 'Say That Again', with its swelling melody and structure that could easily have emerged out of the Karekare valley; and the autumnally serene 'English Trees', which contemplates grief over the simple passing of time (and possibly the loss of Hester). The closer, 'People Are Like Suns,' is among Finn's greatest songs – a piece inspired by Ian McEwan's novel *Saturday* that again can be read as a reflection on transience and the brief candle that is 'time on earth'. These songs are a mournful echo of *Together Alone* and represent the closest Finn has come to the Karekare feeling in the years since the album was made.

Dispossession

Finn has on multiple occasions named *Together Alone* as his favourite Crowded House album.[2] He has, though, also spoken of how it presented difficulties in terms of professional and personal relationships, and that not all memories of the two-month recording period are fond ones; it would be remiss not to acknowledge this. Finn has paid tribute to Youth for his role at Karekare and for undoubtedly expanding the band's capacities, but some of this stress revolved around the English producer.

The difference in work ethic between Finn and Youth was stark, which caused frustration at times (at one point, Youth

---

[2] For a summary of the album's critical reception, and its sales performance, see the ever-reliable *Something So Strong*.

fell asleep as Finn was attempting a vocal). Bourke also quotes Finn suggesting Youth was taking advantage of a lucrative opportunity and that there was a 'cynical edge' to the situation (1997: 255). Finn echoed this in 2016, describing Youth and engineer Greg Hunter as 'hard-edged London wasters' (Neilfinn.com 2016). He spoke in stronger terms in 2021: 'Whatever those magical elements were in his brain, they didn't turn out to be particularly positive, to my mind. We ended up thinking he was a bit of a chancer really … I was pretty dark on Youth after the album.' Seymour went further still, saying, 'I came away from that record feeling completely dispossessed of a lot of things, and it's taken me many years to recover from that experience. I'm still holding a grudge against Youth' (Fangradio 2021a).

For his part, on the few occasions Youth has spoken about producing Crowded House, it has been in generally positive terms. He once cryptically described what he learned from the project as 'unconditional love' (Bourke 1997: 353). In 2022, he spoke with pride about the fact that *Together Alone* is widely regarded as Crowded House's best album, and about how he saw the band as making 'their *Dark Side of the Moon*' (*Rockonteurs* 2022). In an eyebrow-raising interview in 2014, he recalled getting on well with Seymour, visiting a cave where '5000 skulls were piled up' and how LSD was consumed at Karekare (which is, of course, possible, but no other participant in the album has mentioned this in accounts of its making). He also stated how the house/studio, with its floor-to-ceiling outlook onto the valley, inspired him in the design of his own studio in Spain (Berces).

There were plenty of heated moments during recording, involving screaming matches and even the furious throwing around of equipment (Bourke 1997: 255). This fractiousness cannot be entirely attributed to clashes with Youth: the band's fabric was fraying before they even arrived at Karekare after the *Woodface* ordeal, and Finn has admitted that the making of *Together Alone* brought to the surface the personal and musical issues that eventually led him to disband Crowded House in 1996 (Fangradio 2021a). He also said:

> There was a lot of contrary emotion, a loss of innocence in some ways. It felt like in the course of allowing other versions of our band to exist it opened up some slightly darker aspects … and that was always there – Paul in particular. No one that funny doesn't have a fairly dark side and from that record on he was more prone to descending into quite antisocial states of mind. I don't blame the record particularly but I think it did open up and expose the band a bit more, for better or worse.
>
> (Interview 2013)

On several occasions, when discussing the album over the years, he has pointed out that the relationships or marriages of several people in and around the band ruptured on the back of the album's making. It is also significant that Finn has not recorded an album in the same way – in isolation, in residency, as a kind of retreat – since *Together Alone*.

Whether or not this friction produced an energy that served the record's creation is hard to gauge, but that may well have been the case. Either way, it is part of an overarching portrait of the album – something that extends into more areas than this book can cover. For example, some very strong songs were recorded that did not make the final selection, such as 'You Can Touch', 'I Am in Love' and 'Newcastle Jam'. Maybe one or more of these could or should have been included – in place of 'Locked Out', potentially. Another point of debate revolves around the mixing by the revered Bob Clearmountain, which Finn believes tidied up the wilder aspects of the recording and gave it a 'sheen of sophistication it didn't initially have' (Interview 2013).³ There might be scope one day to release a remixed, remastered version of the album with the looser, experimental elements reinstated. There is room to develop further, in a more ethnomusicological context, the significance of what Crowded House attempted with the fusion of traditions on 'Together Alone'. The death of Hester in 2005 cast a new shade over *Together Alone*, with it being his last album with the band, and a thorough tribute to his elite musicianship – with a focus on this record – is also overdue.

Neil Finn and literary symbolism is a topic that *Together Alone* opens too. In one of his Fangradio web broadcasts in 2020, Finn recited lines from the poem 'My Bohemian Existence' by French symbolist poet Arthur Rimbaud. The fact that he pronounced the poet's name slightly incorrectly suggests Finn is not a devotee of Rimbaud. However, several songs on *Together Alone* present dreamy visions, twisted sensory perception and a longing to be in transcendent union with the natural world – all of which are in line with Rimbaud and his late-nineteenth-century symbolist peers. Here is another avenue worthy of more analysis.

A psychogeographic consideration of *Together Alone* and Karekare can be expanded in different ways, such as by diving

---

³ American Clearmountain, a giant of record-making whose stature has only grown since *Together Alone*, had mixed *Woodface* and *Temple of Low Men*. Finn also said of the mixing: 'Youth was very clear and emphatic to work with Clearmountain, I think he admired that we had worked with him before and he was really keen to follow that up. It was also this little insurance policy I think: he thought he could take it right out there, and when Bob comes in he can clean it up' (Interview 2013).

deeper into Māori themes and history. There is also a largely unrecognized strain of ecopoetics in Finn's music. A particular lyrical mode for the expression of environment and wilderness, and humanity's place in it, appears to have been spawned for Finn at Karekare, which has been enduring. As for Karekare as a place of pilgrimage: to this day, many visitors are attracted there by the Crowded House connection – a testament to the fact that *Together Alone* will forever be closely entwined with this landscape, and how an understanding of one is enriched by an understanding of the other.

Grace

The art of songwriting is inherently mysterious, unpredictable and often frustrating. It is something Finn spoke of in his Yale talk, and indeed two songs on *Together Alone* – 'Private Universe' and 'In My Command' – can be read as alluding to this enigma. There is that Leonard Cohen quote, too: 'If I knew where songs came from I would go there more often … The real song, where that comes from, no one knows' (נועם בר שלום).

The most effective and affecting songs are built, I believe, on two parts. Fifty per cent of a song is constructed from straightforward musical ingredients that are technically and theoretically identifiable: notes and chords, harmonic and melodic structures and formulas, rhythms, and indeed the semantic and semiotic addition of words. But a song can't exist on this alone. The other 50 per cent is an intangible and evasive quality from the unconscious, the ether, the heart, the 'universal energy' (or qi) – whatever you want to call it (Cohen called it 'grace'). It is from this that a song gets its life force, its penetration – and here is the shared territory where song and listener meet and form their emotional connection. This section of a song's make-up takes it beyond music into something else – it becomes pure feeling, pure colour, pure heart, pure art. Things in the practical realm of music, like sound and time, seem to fall away.

It is possible for a songwriter to have too much of one and not enough of the other; in his finest work, Finn has the balance in perfect equilibrium. Out of this come Crowded House Moments. The majority of songs on *Together Alone* draw on this 'grace' in a way that takes the album beyond the nuts and bolts of music. To know this album intimately is to cease to hear an instrumental and compositional undertaking made up of disparate parts and people, and to hear it as feeling alone.

As I trundled along with the writing and research for this book, I found myself waiting for the moment when I became thoroughly sick of the album. It never came. I believe this is due to the fact that it transcends the audio experience in this way. This makes it timeless, clearly existing outside of trends and movements. It also gives the album humanity: Cohen's 'grace', as channelled on *Together Alone*, is surely universal, relatable, and accessible to all.

All this said, *Together Alone* is also inscrutable, its essence hidden – and this duality is part of its nature and its allure. In November 2022, I saw the new line-up of Crowded House perform in Sydney. On the packed tram ride home, scores of passengers in my carriage spontaneously began singing the band's songs in unison and did not let up for thirty minutes. It was a lovely thing to witness, but not one of these songs was from *Together Alone*. It is not an album for celebration, for sing-alongs, for communal expression – it is to be experienced alone and remains, to a degree, fascinatingly unknowable.

Also, while writing this book, I visited an exhibition of paintings by the great American artist Philip Guston. A quote of his practically leapt off the wall amid my thinking about exactly what *Together Alone* is: 'Marvellous artists are made of elements which cannot be identified. The alchemy is complete. Their work is strange, and will never become familiar' (Guston 2011: 313).

And this is to return to that Fernando Pessoa poem, 'Song': the secrecy, strangeness and alchemy of the most moving music, and the sublime impossibility of union with it. In a quite visionary way, going to Karekare to make *Together Alone* was Crowded House's own attempt to 'live inside the song' as creators. The result is a record full of songs you want to live inside. To be cocooned within.

Acknowledgements

I wish to acknowledge the Traditional Owners of the land on which this book was written and researched, the Darug and Gundungurra peoples, and pay respects to Elders past, present and future. I extend this respect to all Aboriginal and Torres Strait Islander peoples and acknowledge that sovereignty was never ceded.

I also wish to acknowledge ngā iwi Māori as the Tangata Whenua of Aotearoa and the Te Kawerau ā Maki as the Tangata Whenua of the land on which *Together Alone* was recorded.

Thank you to the 33 1/3 Oceania editors, particularly Jon Dale, for his expertise, encouragement and patience throughout the process – I could not have asked for a more approachable and thoughtful collaborator. Thanks also to Jon Stratton for his assistance, and to Rachel Moore of Bloomsbury Academic in New York.

My heartfelt gratitude goes to Sir Bob Harvey, whose guidance, knowledge, enthusiasm, generosity of spirit and hospitality at Karekare had a major impact on this project and on me.

I wish to thank Romola Smith for her crucial assistance with basic music theory in the analysis of *Together Alone*'s songs, her splendid gifts of interpretation, and her patience with a protracted back-and-forth over the time signature of 'Pineapple Head'.

Huge thanks to Gill Smith and Oliver Downes for reading the manuscript at various stages and for providing sage advice at critical times.

For various miscellaneous but important things, thanks to Jeremy Ansell, Nicola Hart, Dr Toby Martin, Camille Sanson, Karekare Landcare and Piha Community Library.

Thanks to my mother for her love, support and sympathy over many years. Thanks to Julia for too many things to mention here.

This book is dedicated to Tamlin and Arthur: I don't pretend to know what you want, but I offer love.

The author and publisher gratefully acknowledge the permission granted to reproduce the copyrighted material in this book.

Every effort has been made to trace copyright holders and to obtain their permission for the use of copyright material. However, if any have been inadvertently overlooked, the publishers will be pleased, if notified of any omissions, to make the necessary arrangements at the first opportunity.

The third-party copyrighted material displayed in the pages of this book is done so on the basis of 'fair dealing for the purposes of criticism and review' or 'fair use for the purposes of teaching, criticism, scholarship or research' only in accordance with international copyright laws, and is not intended to infringe upon the ownership rights of the original owners.

References

Arvidson, K. (1997), 'Looping de Loop in Lone Kauri Road', *New Zealand Review of Books*, 31 (Spring). Available online: https://nzbooks.org.nz/1997/literature/looping-de-loop-in-lone-kauri-road-ken-arvidson/ (accessed 10 November 2023).

Beaumont, M. ([2001] 2005), 'Neil Finn: One Nil', *NME*, 12 September. Available online: https://www.nme.com/reviews/reviews-nme-4642-337549 (accessed 27 October 2023).

Berces, T. (2014), 'Nobody Does It Like O.Z.O.R.A', 21 August. Available online: https://ozorianprophet.eu/music/nobody-does-it-like-o-z-o-r-a/ (accessed 15 November 2023).

Billingsley, J. (2017), 'The City and the Country: Psychogeography – as We See It', *Northern Earth Magazine*, September: 13–18. Available online: https://northernearth.co.uk/the-city-and-the-country/ (accessed 10 November 2023).

Bourke, C. (1997), *Crowded House: Something So Strong*, Sydney: Pan Macmillan.

Cody Carvel (2018), 'USA: Poetry Episode Anne Sexton', YouTube, 25 December. https://www.youtube.com/watch?v=ONIpxRPFv3k.

Crowded House (1994), *Together Alone – Piano/Vocal/Guitar*, Woodford Green: International Music Publications Limited.

Crowded House (2021), 'Nails in My Feet', on *Live 92–94 Part 2*, Black Box Records, streaming audio, Spotify.

Crowded House Live! (2009), 'Crowded House on Much Music More Questions and Banter (11/13)', YouTube, 28 April. https://www.youtube.com/watch?v=bNYFlWpybrI&t=69s.

Curnow, A. (1997), *Early Days Yet: New and Collected Poems, 1941–1997*, Auckland: Auckland University Press.

Debord, G. E. ([1955] n.d.), 'Introduction to a Critique of Urban Geography', online publication. Available online: http://library.nothingness.org/articles/SI/en/display/2 (accessed 29 July 2024).

Debord, G. E. ([1956] n.d.), 'Theory of the Dérive', trans. K. Knabb, online publication. Available online: http://library.nothingness.org/articles/all/en/display/314 (accessed 29 July 2024).

Denselow, R. (1989), *When the Music's Over: The Story of Political Pop*, London: Faber & Faber.

Doyle, T. (2009), 'Youth: From Killing Joke to Paul McCartney', *Sound on Sound*, March. Available online: https://www.soundonsound.com/people/youth-killing-joke-paul-mccartney (accessed 9 November 2023).

Fangradio (2021a), 'Album by Album: Together Alone', podcast, 1 April. https://www.fangradio.com/episodes/crowded-house-together-alone.

Fangradio (2021b), 'Album by Album: Woodface', podcast, 4 March. https://www.fangradio.com/episodes/crowded-house-album-by-album-woodface.

Finn, N. (2013), interview by Barnaby Smith, Sydney, 17 March.

Finn, N. (2023), 'Storms', Neilfinn.com, 17 February. Available online: https://www.neilfinn.com/journal/2023/2/17/hjhrum84o6vabtlkjjvnh24ciskalm.

Frame, J. (1985), *The Envoy from Mirror City*, New York: George Braziller.

Frame, J. ([2007] 2009), *Towards Another Summer*, Berkeley, CA: Counterpoint.

Garland, E. (2016), 'We Interviewed a Druid about Glastonbury', *Vice*, 23 June. Available online: https://www.vice.com/en/article/rkqd3e/we-interviewed-a-druid-about-glastonbury (accessed 9 November 2023).

Green, P. (2016a), 'Together Alone – Crowded House filmed @ kare kare', YouTube, 7 September. https://www.youtube.com/watch?v=mhDlyWxMqlc (accessed 1 November 2023).

Green, P. (2016b), 'Crowded House Catherine Wheels Corner 96', YouTube, https://www.youtube.com/watch?v=tk5zVkre87g (accessed 13 November 2023).

Guston, P. (2011), *Philip Guston: Collected Writings, Lectures, and Conversations*, ed. Clark Coolidge, Berkeley, CA: University of California Press.

Harvey, B. (2001), *Rolling Thunder: The Spirit of Karekare*, Auckland: Exisle.

Harvey, B. (2023), interview by Barnaby Smith, online, 10 February.

Harvey, B. (n.d.), 'Karekare, The Gathering Place', quoted in 'History of the Waitakere Ranges', Waitakere Ranges Protection Society. Available online: https://waitakereranges.org.nz/about-the-ranges/history-of-the-waitakere-ranges/ (accessed 10 November 2023).

Hepburn, G. (2011), 'Pillars of the Community', *New Zealand Herald*, 1 October: G3.

Holden, S. (1991), 'Rock and Pop in Review', *New York Times*, 10 October. Available online: https://www.nytimes.com/1991/10/10/arts/pop-and-jazz-in-review-828991.html (accessed 27 October 2023).

James, J. (1995), 'Remembrance of Musical Things Past', *New York Times*, 19 November. Available online: https://www.nytimes.com/1995/11/19/books/remembrance-of-musical-things-past.html (accessed 18 October 2023).

MacDonald, I. (1995), *Revolution in the Head: The Beatles' Records and the Sixties*, London: Pimlico.

Made By Music (2023), 'Ep10: Youth', podcast, 12 July. https://open.spotify.com/episode/6NCBcn5xTnrRUXc636dVp5?si=3e88c6e2ae3d48fa.

Marr, D. (1991), *Patrick White: The Life*, Sydney: Random House Australia.

McClure, T. (2023), 'Cyclone Gabrielle Worst Storm to Hit New Zealand This Century, Says PM', *The Guardian*, 14 February. Available online: https://www.theguardian.com/world/2023/feb/13/cyclone-gabrielle-new-zealand-declares-national-state-of-emergency.

Mitchell, T. (2009), 'Sonic Psychogeography: A Poetics of Place in Popular Music in Aotearoa/New Zealand', *Perfect Beat*, 10: 145–75.

Moorhouse, G. (2008), 'Cold Comfort', *The Guardian*, 5 July. Available online: https://www.theguardian.com/books/2008/jul/05/saturdayreviewsfeatres.guardianreview23 (accessed 3 November 2023).

Neil Finn (2012), 'Crowded House – Locked Out (Live at Fleadh 1994)', YouTube, 12 May. https://www.youtube.com/watch?v=EDj2DqcDAS4.

Neil Finn (2018), 'Neil Finn's Home Demo Studio, 1991', YouTube, 24 June. https://www.youtube.com/watch?v=nKf3VsWGnr8.

Neilfinn.com (2016), '"Above and Beneath": Neil Finn and Nick Seymour Talk about the Making of Together Alone', audio interview, https://www.neilfinn.com/together-alone.

Neilfinn.com (n.d. a), 'Catherine Wheels', Available online: https://www.neilfinn.com/catherine-wheels (accessed 13 November 2023).

Neilfinn.com (n.d. b), 'Distant Sun', Available online: https://www.neilfinn.com/distant-sun (accessed 13 November 2023).

Neilfinn.com (n.d. c), 'Locked Out', Available online: https://www.neilfinn.com/locked-out (accessed 13 November 2023).

Neilfinn.com (n.d. d), 'Skin Feeling', Available online: https://www.neilfinn.com/skin-feeling (accessed 13 November 2023).

New Zealand Government (2014), *Te Kawerau a Maki and the Trustees of Te Kawerau Iwi Settlement Trust and the Crown: Deed of Settlement of Historical Claims*, 22 February. Available online: https://www.www.govt.nz/assets/Documents/OTS/Te-Kawerau-a-Maki/Te-Kawerau-a-Maki-Deed-of-Settlement.pdf (accessed 10 November 2023).

NME (1997), 'Radiohead Back in the USA', 27 October. Available online: https://www.nme.com/news/music/radiohead-1018-1394418 (accessed 4 November 2023).

O'Brien, G. (2018), 'Some Remarks on Poetry and the Environment in Aotearoa/New Zealand', *Poetry*, 1 February. Available online: https://www.poetryfoundation.org/poetrymagazine/articles/145497/some-remarks-on-poetry-and-the-environment-in-aotearoa-new-zealand (accessed 10 November 2023).

O'Sullivan, V. (2018), 'The Nietzsche of Lone Kauri Road: The Life and Verse of Allen Curnow', *The Spinoff*, 24 January. Available online: https://thespinoff.co.nz/

books/24-01-2018/the-nietzsche-of-lone-kauri-road-the-life-and-verse-of-allen-curnow.

Overall, J. (2016), 'Walking Backwards: Psychogeographical Approaches to Heritage', paper presented at *CHAT2016: Rurality, University of the Highlands and Islands, Kirkwall, Orkney*, 21–3 October, Available online: https://repository.canterbury.ac.uk/download/005306819e546adf00906effc9c1ea1e18ad2e0025839c0336645381971a3a32/369052/15087.pdf (accessed 1 November 2023).

Paphides, P. (1996), liner notes to *Recurring Dream*, Crowded House, compact disc, Capitol Records.

Pessoa, F. (1982), *Selected Poems*, 2nd edn, trans. J. Griffin, London: Penguin.

Pro Audio Asia (2009), 'Karekare and Fairlight, Pioneers Together', March–April. Available online: http://www.thenotepad.com.au/uploads/PAA%20News_pp10.pdf (accessed 4 November 2023).

Proust, M. ([1913] 1970), *Swann's Way*, trans. C. K. Scott Moncrieff, New York: Vintage.

Proust, M. ([1949] 2006), *Letters of Marcel Proust*, ed. and trans. M. Curtiss, New York: Helen Marks Books, Books & Co.

Rockonteurs with Gary Kemp and Guy Pratt (2022), 'S2E24: Youth', 19 June. https://play.acast.com/s/rockonteurs-with-gary-kemp-and-guy-pratt/s2e24-youth.

Ruskin, J. (1856), 'Of the Pathetic Fallacy', *Modern Painters Vol. III. Containing Part IV., Of Many Things*, Project Gutenberg eBook: 152–67. Available online: https://www.gutenberg.org/files/38923/38923-h/38923-h.htm#CHAPTER_XII.

Sacks, O. (2017), *The River of Consciousness*, London: Picador.

Smith, B. (2014), 'Effort for Effortlessness: Neil Finn's Baker's Dozen', *The Quietus*, 30 January. Available online: https://thequietus.

com/articles/14392-neil-finn-favourite-albums (accessed 29 October 2023).

Stern, M. J. (2014), 'Neural Nostalgia: Why Do We Love the Music We Heard as Teenagers?', *Slate*, 12 August. Available online: https://slate.com/technology/2014/08/musical-nostalgia-the-psychology-and-neuroscience-for-song-preference-and-the-reminiscence-bump.html (accessed 18 October 2023).

Stuff (2009), 'Sir Ed's Bach a Place of Solace', 18 February. Available online: https://www.stuff.co.nz/auckland/local-news/nor-west-news/219062/Sir-Eds-bach-a-place-of-solace (accessed 4 November 2023).

Taonui, R. (2017), 'Tamaki Tribes', *The Encyclopedia of New Zealand*, 22 March. Available online: https://teara.govt.nz/en/tamaki-tribes/print (accessed 10 November 2023).

Te Kawerau ā Maki (2023), email message to author, 15 October.

Te Kawerau ā Maki (n.d.), 'About Us', Available online: https://tekawerau.iwi.nz/about-us/ (accessed 10 November 2023).

The Institute of Art and Ideas (2020), 'Will Self / Psychogeography', YouTube, 21 August, https://www.youtube.com/watch?v=yPqTCKtbBBA.

Thompson, A. (n.d.), 'C14 Reviews', *Planet Mellotron*, Available online: https://www.planetmellotron.com/revc14.htm (accessed 13 November 2023).

WTF with Marc Maron (2016), 'Paul Dano / Adam Goldberg', podcast, 11 July, http://www.wtfpod.com/podcast/episode-723-paul-dano-adam-goldberg.

Wynn, K. (2011), 'Famous People Passed His Way', *New Zealand Herald*, 3 December. Available online: https://www.nzherald.co.nz/nz/famous-people-passed-his-way/3VC2IZA4MMO6UKE5BILQCI64TY/ (accessed 4 November 2023).

Yale School of Medicine (2017), 'Psychiatry Grand Rounds 09/21/2012 v. 2.0', Vimeo, 8 August, https://vimeo.com/228999830.

Young, R. (2010), *Electric Eden: Unearthing Britain's Visionary Music*, London: Faber & Faber.

שלום בר נועם (2017), 'Leonard Cohen on Israeli TV, 1985, a rare interview', YouTube, 8 November, https://www.youtube.com/watch?v=dZdQCv38Jao.

Index

20 Karekare Road 32–3, 61–2

Afterglow 35, 89
album art, *see under* Seymour, Nick

Band, The 22
Beatles, The 13, 80, 84, 101
'Black and White Boy' 48, 80–2, 85, 89
Blake, Tchad 36, 48
Bowie, David 40, 84
Boyd, Arthur 29
Britpop 14, 15, 16
Brontë, Emily 94–5

Carey, Peter 86
'Catherine Wheels' 5, 23, 45, 77, 92–5
'Chocolate Cake' 6, 7, 17, 71, 96
Clearmountain, Bob 105–6
Cohen, Leonard 107–8
Coleman, Jaz 32
Cook Islands log drummers 45, 89, 96
Crowded House (album) 10
Crowded House Moments 4–5, 108
Curnow, Allen 64–7, 69, 70

Debord, Guy 27, 54–6
'dérive' 56, 62, 65

'Distant Sun' 47, 80, 91–2
'Don't Dream It's Over' 7, 18, 35, 39, 72, 78, 92, 96

Fairport Convention 23
'Fall at Your Feet' 6, 16
'Fingers of Love' 23, 47, 68, 82–3, 84
Finn 74, 101, 102
Finn, Neil 3, 4, 5, 6–7, 8, 13, 24, 35, 49, 102, 108
    attitude towards New Zealand 28–31
    fusion with Māori music 97–8
    lyrical style 10–1, 20, 71–3, 79–80, 84–5, 87–8, 96, 106
    media reaction to Crowded House 14
    mumble-singing 5, 75, 80, 92
    on how *Together Alone* affected band 105
    on Karekare 53, 57, 60–1, 69, 70
    on Mark Hart 47–8
    on *Together Alone*'s atmosphere 8, 33
    output after *Together Alone* 101–3
    reasons for recording at Karekare 17, 18–21, 26–7

relationship with Youth 37, 38–9, 39–40, 42, 43, 44, 45, 90, 101–2, 103–4
seeking location for recording 31–2
sick with giardia 87
singing 5, 76–7, 86–7, 88–9, 90, 91, 97
Finn, Tim 9, 36, 47, 101
songwriting with Neil 6, 19, 20
'Four Seasons in One Day' 4, 6, 16
Frame, Janet 30, 31
Fraternity 22
Froom, Mitchell 6, 9, 17, 20, 39, 43, 47

Guston, Philip 109

Hart, Mark 9, 19, 24, 36, 67, 85
career prior to *Together Alone* 46–7
impression of Youth 43
musicianship 10, 47–8, 74, 80, 81–2, 87, 89, 91, 97
vocal on 'Skin Feeling' 46, 95
Harvey, Sir Bob 57–8, 59, 60, 61, 63, 66, 68, 69, 70
Heron 24–5, 44
Hester, Paul 7, 25, 28, 97
'Black and White Boy' 80–1
death 102, 103, 106
drumming 35–6, 44, 74, 75, 86
on experience at Karekare 26, 33, 60, 69–70

persona on-stage 36
relationship with Youth 40, 45–6
songwriting 35, 95–6
struggles with touring 7, 27–8
Hillary, Sir Edmund 32, 58
'Hole in the River' 35, 72
Horrocks, Jody 25, 32
Horrocks, Nigel 25, 32, 33, 74
Hunter, Greg 26, 104

'In My Command' 5, 25, 48, 52, 76–8, 79, 88, 107
'Into Temptation' 71, 80, 90
'Italian Plastic' 35, 95
'It's Only Natural' 6, 7, 16
jamming 44–5, 73, 93

'Kare Kare' 23, 44, 46, 48, 73–6, 79, 82, 101
Karekare 1, 5, 8, 27, 49, 68–9, 98, 99, 103, 106–7, 109
Cyclone Gabrielle impact 62–3
effect of landscape on band 10–1, 20–1, 27, 86, 92
isolation of 17, 25
Karekare Beach 9, 51–3, 65
Karekare Falls 61
Māori history 58–61
place of pilgrimage 53–4, 67, 107
weather conditions 52, 69–70, 81, 83
Killing Joke 32, 37, 38, 39

Led Zeppelin 22
Lennon, John 71, 85
Lillywhite, Steve 38, 39
'Locked Out' 44, 48, 57, 85–7, 89, 95

McCartney, (Sir) Paul 38, 40, 71
'My Telly's Gone Bung' 35

'Nails in My Feet' 4, 44, 47, 78–80
Ngāpuhi (tribe) 59, 60, 74

One Nil 19, 101
outdoor recording 24–5, 44, 91

Pajama Club 14, 19
Paphides, Peter 3–4, 15
Paratahi Island 51, 63
pathetic fallacy 67–8
Patterson, Andrew 32
Pessoa, Fernando 3, 11, 109
'Pineapple Head' 24, 48, 83–5, 86, 92
'Private Universe' 23, 46, 48, 68, 86, 87–9, 107
Proust, Marcel 3
psychedelia 19, 39, 43, 46, 75, 87, 91
psychogeography 11, 27, 54–7, 64, 65, 67, 106–7

Rangi and Papa (myth) 9, 98
Rayner, Eddie 36
record label expectations 6, 86
Recurring Dream 4, 16
Rimbaud, Arthur 106
Rosselson, Leon 18

Rousseau, Jean-Jacques 55
Ruskin, John 67

Sacks, Oliver 20
Self, Will 55, 56–7
Seven Worlds Collide 14, 19
Seymour, Nick 7, 19, 20, 24, 28, 90, 102
   album art 48–50
   bass playing 4, 5, 35–6, 44, 46, 77, 80, 84, 93
   on-stage persona 36
   relationship with Youth 40, 45, 104
'Silent House' 21, 72
'Skin Feeling' 46, 95–6
Split Enz 46, 92

Tame Impala 22, 25
Te Kawerau ā Maki (tribe) 58–61, 74
Te Matua (The Watchman) 9, 51, 53, 59, 63–4, 74
Te Tokapiri (Tom Thumb Rock) 63–4
Te Waka Huia Cultural Group Choir 45, 77, 93, 96–7
Temple of Low Men 6, 10, 46, 71, 74, 84
The Fireman 38, 40
The Piano 32, 64
Thompson, Richard 23, 48
Thoreau, Henry David 26
Time On Earth 21, 102–3
'Together Alone' 48, 61, 96–9
Traffic 22–3, 25
Try Whistling This 18, 101, 102

Waitakere (region) 8, 58, 59, 60
'Walking on the Spot' 5, 48, 89–91
'Weather With You' 4, 6, 7, 16, 72, 78, 92
Wehi, Bub 97, 98
Wharengarahi (cave) 59, 61, 74
'Whispers and Moans' 35, 78
White, Patrick 29
Williams, Fred 29
Wilson, Brian 87
Woodface 9, 13, 19, 35, 39, 75, 84, 92, 95, 105
    contrast with *Together Alone* 8, 10, 16–18, 74, 91
    making of 6–7
    touring and promotion 27, 45, 47
'World Where You Live' 4, 78

Young, Neil 19, 44
Youth (Martin Glover) 1, 9, 19, 20, 26, 32, 36, 74, 90
    career prior to *Together Alone* 37–41
    contributions to *Together Alone* 9, 10, 24, 73, 75, 81, 86, 88, 92, 97, 101, 103–5
    meeting Crowded House 39–40
    paganism 9, 41–2, 49, 61
    production style 23, 42–6